ASTRONOMY

DANTES/DSST* Test Study Guide

All rights reserved. This Study Guide, Book and Flashcards are protected under the US Copyright Law. No part of this book or study guide or flashcards may be reproduced, distributed or stored in a retrieval system, or transmitted in any form or by any means, electronic, mechanical, photocopying, recording, or otherwise, without the prior written permission of the publisher Breely Crush Publishing, LLC.

© 2026 Breely Crush Publishing, LLC

DSST is a registered trademark of The Thomson Corporation and its affiliated companies, and does not endorse this book.

971010620143

Copyright ©2003 - 2026, Breely Crush Publishing, LLC.

All rights reserved.

This Study Guide, Book and Flashcards are protected under the US Copyright Law. No part of this publication may be reproduced, distributed or stored in a retrieval system, or transmitted in any form or by any means, electronic, mechanical, photocopying, recording, or otherwise, without the prior written permission of the publisher Breely Crush Publishing, LLC.

Published by Breely Crush Publishing, LLC
10808 River Front Parkway
South Jordan, UT 84095
www.breelycrushpublishing.com

ISBN-10: 1-61433-657-1
ISBN-13: 978-1-61433-657-0

Printed and bound in the United States of America.

*DSST is a registered trademark of The Thomson Corporation and its affiliated companies, and does not endorse this book.

Table of Contents

Introduction to the Science of Astronomy 1
    Nature of Science 1
    How Scientists Think and Work 1
    History of Early Astronomy 2
    History of the Telescope 4
Cosmic Forces 6
    Motion 6
    Gravity 14
    Energy 16
    Relativity 20
Celestial Systems 23
    Earth and the Sky 23
    Earth and the Moon 27
    Time and the Calendar 32
The Science of Light 34
    The Electromagnetic System 34
    Measurement and Analysis of Light 41
Planetary Systems: Our Solar System and Others 43
    Contents of Our Solar System 43
    Planets Outside of Our Solar System 59
Our Galaxy and Other Galaxies: Contents and Structure 60
    Our Galaxy: The Milky Way 60
    Other Galaxies and Galaxy Clusters 72
    Cosmic Distances 75
The Universe: Contents, Structure and Evolution 76
    Large-Scale Structure 76
Life in the Universe 86
    Extremes of Life on Earth 86
    Life in the Solar System 88
    Life Beyond the Solar System 89
Sample Test Questions 91
Test Taking Strategies 127
What Your Score Means 127
Test Preparation 128
Legal Note 129

Introduction to the Science of Astronomy

NATURE OF SCIENCE

In the general sense, "science" can be described as a process of seeking further understanding of processes and laws by which the natural world is governed. Science seeks to find reliable and consistent explanations to questions. In this sense, the field of science is inherently limited matters which can be objectively studied. Anything that is subjective, ethical, religious, or political is without the realm of scientific explanation. Scientific knowledge is also inherently tentative. Laws are descriptions of known truths. Theories are proposed explanations to the existence of those laws. As time and experimentation are applied to theories they are either proven to have merit, or to be pure speculation. In either case, scientific knowledge is continually growing and increasing as the search for truth continues.

HOW SCIENTISTS THINK AND WORK

Although scientific methods are often used to describe the basics of the process, there is no single correct process by which discoveries are made. While certain aspects of scientific inquiry are typically present, each new problem requires its own solution. Some of the most common steps in the scientific process are developing a question, research, hypothesis, testing and observation, analysis, and forming a conclusion.

Questioning is the basis for all scientific discovery. Progress is not made until someone has a question. While the development of a question is an open-ended pursuit, it is important that good questions are asked in order for good experiments and discoveries to be made. Furthermore, extensive research is an important stage of the scientific method. Once a question is developed, research is conducted to determine what is already known about the question. For example, have others already proposed answers to the question? Can the answer be determined without further experimentation? What background information about the question or problem is already known?

As a person researches various aspects of their question, they will be able to develop a hypothesis. A hypothesis is much more than simply an educated guess. Rather, it is the best possible explanation that exists at the time. A good hypothesis is testable, and can be disproven if it is false. Once the hypothesis has been made, then experimentation can begin. In some cases this phase requires testing of some nature. In other cases observation is all that is required.

Once testing and observation have been completed, all that remains is to analyze the data and come to a conclusion. Often further observations may be needed, or alterations to the hypothesis will be made to allow for further study and experimentation. The process repeats and refines until a theory can be developed.

HISTORY OF EARLY ASTRONOMY

Astronomy is one of the earliest branches of science. Essentially since the beginning of mankind, people have looked to the stars and wondered about their place in the universe. Knowledge of the stars was used for both practical purposes – such as navigation, prediction of eclipses, and tracking time – and for religious purposes. The human understanding of the universe is an excellent example of how the scientific process works. Each successive generation of astronomers built on the work of their predecessors and colleagues. As knowledge and scientific understanding grew, it allowed the development of more refined and accurate models.

Early theories about the structure of the universe were varied. Some theorized that the Earth was a flat disc suspended in an endless ocean. Others believed that each star and planet existed in its own sphere and that when the spheres overlapped a celestial melody could be heard. Still others argued that the stars were fixed in their place in a bowl-shaped expanse that stretched over a flat Earth.

Although others before him had made the argument that the Earth was round, Aristotle is given credit for popularizing and solidifying this view. Aristotle was so well known and respected that his ideas were taught and believed for centuries. In the 4th century BC, Aristotle argued a geocentric model of the universe. Geocentric models are models in which the Earth is believed to be at the center of the solar system. Aristotle believed the Earth and stars to be perfect spheres. He claimed that each planet existed within its own sphere comprised of a divine element known as aether which he claimed moved in a naturally circular direction. Because the planets were suspended in these spheres it accounted for their circular rotations around the Earth. Aristotle also argued the existence of a "Prime Mover" which set all of the spheres in motion.

The largest problem with Aristotle's model was that it couldn't account for the observable retrograde movement of many stars. In other words, it was clear based on changes in the brightness of many stars that at certain times they were moving away from the Earth. This problem was solved with a solution proposed by Claudius Ptolemy in the 1st century AD. Ptolemy sustained Aristotle's claim of a geocentric model of the solar system, and also maintained that all stars and planets moved in perfect, circular patterns. However, he added several aspects to the theory in order to make it mathematically consistent. Firstly, Ptolemy argued that planets orbited not only in perfect circles, but that they also moved in epicycles within those orbits. In other words, rather than a single large circular orbit, according to Ptolemy the planets were making small, perfect circular movements within their overall circular orbit. The second addition to Aristotle's theory that Ptolemy claimed was that the Earth was not directly in the center of the planets' orbits. Rather it was slightly offset at an eccentric point. Thirdly, Ptolemy argued that there was an "equant." This was essentially a theoretical point within the solar system from which the planetary motion could be observed to be uniform.

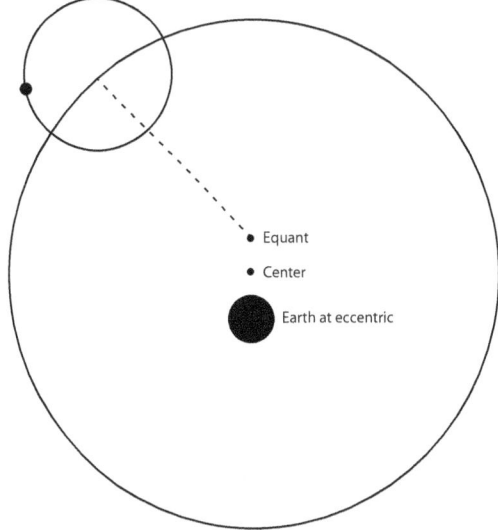

The virtue of Ptolemy's theory was that it made Aristotle's model mathematically feasible. This allowed science to continue to maintain the belief that the Earth was at the center of the universe, and that planetary movement occurred through perfect circular motions. Although both of these beliefs were eventually proven false, the respect that existed for these two philosophers was strong enough that it continued without serious challenge for nearly 1,500 years.

Nicolaus Copernicus was the first to challenge the geocentric models of Aristotle and Ptolemy. Rather than placing the Earth at the center of the solar system, Copernicus claimed that the Sun was at the center of the solar system. This model is known as a heliocentric model. Copernicus' main criticism of the geocentric model was that it was too complex to have occurred naturally. The theory of epicycles to explain retrograde motion sometimes required as many as seven different epicycles – or orbits with orbits – to be mathematically feasible. In 1514 Copernicus published his book arguing that the retrograde motion was much more easily explained by a heliocentric model of the solar system. His book also correctly explained that the rising and setting of the Sun was due to Earth's own rotation, and that the Earth's own motion accounted for the retrograde movement of the stars. Although Copernicus' model was not perfect – it still claimed perfect circular orbits – it was a major step in astronomical understanding.

Following Copernicus, the next major developments in astronomy are attributed to Tycho Brahe – a Danish astronomer who lived in the 16th century. Brahe is credited with building the first dedicated observatory – despite the fact that the telescope had still not been invented. Brahe proposed a model of the solar system that integrated both the Copernican view and that of Aristotle. He theorized that while the five other known planets in the solar system revolved around the Sun, the Sun and the Moon revolved around the Earth. The theory became a popular middle ground between the traditional views and Aristotle and the radical views of Copernicus. Brahe is also known for building the first true observatory from which he made observations and kept records that were instrumental to future discoveries. Brahe was the first person to observe a supernova. Although he believed that it was the creation of a new star and not the explosion of an existing one, it was proof that the heavens did change. This contradicted the traditional views that the heavens were constant and unchanging.

Around the time of Brahe's death, Galileo Galilei began making great strides in observation by constructing a telescope. Prior to Galileo the vast majority of astronomical observation had been done by the naked eye. This is partially the reason why there was so much contention about the true structure of the solar system. The naked eye is simply too weak to measure the tiniest movements amongst the stars. With Galileo's telescope he was able to make groundbreaking discoveries such as the craters in the Moon, Sunspot activities, and four of Jupiter's Moons. The discovery of Moon's orbiting Jupiter was particularly important because it shattered Aristotle's theory that everything orbited only the Earth. Galileo's other observations further proved that celestial bodies were not in fact perfect. Because of his discoveries, Galileo is considered to be the Father of Observational Astronomy. He was put on trial by the Catholic Church for contesting their teachings of a geocentric solar system, and was kept under house arrest for the rest of his life.

In the meantime, Tycho Brahe's work was being continued by his apprentice Johannes Kepler (1571-1630). After Brahe's death, Kepler had inherited his vast records, and he used them to continue studying. While Kepler supported the heliocentric model, he noted that the motion of the planet Mars could not be explained under the model with a perfect circular orbit. Based on Brahe's records, Kepler was able to develop three Laws of Planetary Motion that are still used today. Most importantly Kepler was the first person to claim that planets did not orbit in perfect circular patterns, but rather that they followed elliptical paths.

These theories were all brought together by the work of famous mathematician Sir Isaac Newton (1643-1727) in the following century. Newton developed extensive laws of algebra and calculus that proved the validity of Kepler's laws, and Copernicus's model. Equally importantly, Newton extensively studied the principles of gravity and motion as they worked on the Earth's surface, and showed that the same principles could be applied to planetary motion. With this final piece of the puzzle complete, understanding about the motions of the stars was able to progress rapidly. Scientific though continues to improve and progress today following the same patterns of scientific exploration.

HISTORY OF THE TELESCOPE

The invention of the telescope revolutionized astronomical studies. Although lenses for correcting vision came into fairly common use in the 14th and 15th centuries, the invention of the telescope did not follow for several hundred more years. The earliest documented telescope is credited to Hans Lippershey in the Netherlands. Hans applied for a patent after discovering that he could use two lenses held apart from each other to magnify his view of an object. The patent was denied, but news of his discovery traveled, and the following year, Galileo constructed several telescopes of his own and pointed them towards the skies. Although three-powered telescopes were becoming fairly common by this point, Galileo succeeding in constructing a three-powered telescope, an eight-powered telescope, and finally a twenty-powered telescope which he used to make his critical observations.

Galileo's telescopes were refraction telescopes, meaning that they used concave and convex lenses to bend and magnify light. The objective lens (the one at the far end of the telescope) was convex, meaning that it stuck out towards the object being observed. The ocular lens or eyepiece (the one at the near end of the telescope) was concave. This allowed the image to be brought back into focus and directed it through the eyepiece. The telescopes were about 30-40 inches in length. The design was far from perfect, however. One problem with these telescopes was that the glass had a slight greenish tint because of iron impurities in the glass. Another limitation of the telescopes was their small aperture or field of view. For example, only about a quarter of the Moon could be observed at a time using Galileo's telescope. Despite these early shortcomings, Galileo's design is still one of the most commonly used today.

Refraction telescopes, such as Galileo's are typically discussed in terms of their power. Power is the amount of magnification that the telescope produces. This can be determined based on the focal length of the lenses. The equation for this is

$$Power = \frac{Focal\ Length\ of\ Optical\ Lens}{Focal\ Length\ of\ Eyepiece}$$

For example, with Galileo's telescope, the optical lens had a focal length of approximately 40 inches. The eyepiece had a focal length of approximately 2 inches. Therefore, we know that the telescope that he used to view the stars had a power of 40 inches/2 inches or 20. Power is not the most important aspect of a telescope, however. Simply increasing the power of the magnification can result in blurry or unhelpful images. The fact that Galileo's telescope only showed one quarter of the Moon is an example of this problem. He could have increased the power of the telescope, but it would have restricted his view even further. It's important to find the proper balance between power and aperture. Aperture refers to the diameter of the lenses. As this increases the telescope is able to gather more light and have an expanded field of vision.

After Galileo's use of the refraction telescope, others continued to tinker with the design to create even more clear and accurate telescopes. The first proposed improvement was by Johannes Kepler. Kepler noted that by using two convex lenses instead of the convex and concave combination of Galileo's model, this allowed for increased magnification, but never became particularly popular because it caused the images to be displayed upside down. Another problem with Kepler's model was that the double magnification resulted in color and shape distortion.

The next major development in telescope technology was made by Sir Isaac Newton. Newton recognized that the problems with the Galilean model could all be attributed to the glass. As a solution to the problem, he developed the concept of the reflector telescope which used mirrors instead of glass. Although others had experimented with the use of mirrors in telescopes, Newton was the first to construct a practical model for it. Newton's model used a mirror with a convex curvature that was reflected onto an angled, flat mirror, and directed into a concave lens. The process for creating a convex mirror proved to be incredibly difficult for others to repeat, however, and the telescope required a lot of maintenance. With time, however, others made improvements to the model, including parabolic mirrors in place of spherical ones, and higher quality mirrors.

As time has progressed, even more advancements in telescope technology have come to pass. For example, the Hubble Telescope avoids distortions caused by Earth's atmosphere because it is located in space. Another example is the use of radio telescopes. Unlike traditional telescopes, radio telescopes work by measuring the presence of radio waves rather than visual light. This has several advantages over traditional telescopes. Radio waves are a much longer wave than visible light. As a result, radio waves travel farther through the universe without becoming distorted or absorbed by dust. Magnetic fields are also visible with a radio telescope, which allows them to be much more easily studied. Another important advantage of radio telescopes is that they allow for a view of the universe that is not visible to the human eye. For example, a vast majority of the universe is composed of hydrogen. While hydrogen atoms do not emit energy on the visible light spectrum, some forms are visible through a radio telescope, allowing for the study of objects that are completely invisible to the naked eye. Radio telescopes are also less affected by weather problems, and can be used at any time of day or night. The biggest limitations of radio telescopes is that they experience a high amount of interference from media on the planet Earth, and that due to the size of the radio wavelengths resolution is less clear than traditional telescopes.

Cosmic Forces

MOTION

In scientific terms, motion is described as a change in position over a period of time. The study of motion encompasses everything from the smallest movements within atoms to the large scale movements of the Sun, Moon, and stars. Sir Isaac Newton showed that planetary motion is governed by the same principles that govern movement on Earth. Therefore, in order to understand the motion of the planets, it is important to first understand the basic principles of physics. This includes the concepts of position, speed, velocity, and acceleration.

Motion is always considered relative to an object's position. For this reason it is important to have a frame of reference. For example, imagine watching a shooting star. Relative to the position of a person on Earth, the star is moving quickly across the sky. However, if an individual were standing on that particular star it would appear instead that the Earth were moving quickly across the sky. Furthermore, to an individual in a third location, perhaps another star, both the first star and the planet Earth would appear to be moving while that person stood still. As a result, it is important to know what frame of reference is being used whenever calculations of position come into play. Position is usually denoted by the term "x." For example, x=3 would describe an object with a position of 3.

Speed and velocity are two other important measures of motion. Both speed and velocity are used to describe changes in an object's position. Speed refers to the movement of an object over time. If an object has a high speed then it is moving large distances in a short amount of time. If it has a low speed then it is moving smaller distances in longer periods of time. The equation for speed is:

$$Speed = \frac{Distance}{Time}$$

Velocity is similar to speed because it is similarly a measurement of how quickly an object is moving. The difference is that velocity is also designed to measure the direction in which that object is moving. This is why the frame of reference is important to understand when studying motion. An object with a positive velocity is moving forward. An object with a negative velocity is moving backward. Velocity is usually denoted by the term "v." For example, v=10 m/s, would describe an object moving with a velocity of 10 meters per second. The equation for velocity is:

$$Velocity = \frac{Displacement}{Time} = \frac{x_2 - x_1}{t_2 - t_1}$$

In this equation, displacement refers to the change in an object's position. It can be calculated by subtracting the beginning position from the ending position. Similarly, the amount of time that has passed can be found by subtracting the starting time from the ending time. Typically the starting time will be zero, and the equation can be shortened to simply "t." Velocity is typically measured in units of distance over time. Most commonly it is "meters per second." But feet per second, miles per hour, or other measurements can be used as well.

Acceleration is used to describe changes in an object's velocity. For example, if an object is increasing in speed then it is described as accelerating. This is why the gas pedal on a car is also known as the accelerator – it is responsible for causing changes in the speed, or velocity, of the car. Just as velocity is calculated by determining change in position over a period of time, acceleration is calculated by determining the changes in velocity over a period of time. The equation for acceleration is:

$$Acceleration = \frac{v_2 - v_1}{t_2 - t_1}$$

When an object has a positive acceleration, this means that the object is increasing its velocity. When an object has a negative acceleration it means that the object is decreasing its velocity. It is important to understand that a negative acceleration does not indicate that an object is moving backwards (as it does with velocity). Furthermore, an object can be moving very quickly or very slowly and still have no acceleration at all. Acceleration simply indicates that the velocity is changing. Acceleration is measured in units of distance over time squared. Most commonly it is meters per second squared (m/s2).

Several equations can be used to demonstrate the relationship between these three measures. These are referred to as the kinematic equations. The first of the kinematic equations relates the distance traveled when starting velocity, acceleration, and time are known, but when final velocity is not.

$$d = v_0 t + \frac{1}{2} a t^2$$

If an object is starting from rest, the first term in the equation will always be zero. The following example illustrates how the equation can be used. A car is parked at a stoplight. It begins to accelerate at a rate of 3 meters per second squared for 5 seconds. How far has the car traveled in this time?

In this example, V0 (the initial velocity) is zero because the car is not in motion. Time is 5 seconds, and acceleration is 3 m/s2. Therefore, the problem would be solved as:

$$d = (0)(5) + \frac{1}{2}(3)(5)^2 = 37.5 \, meters$$

The second kinematic equation can be used to solve for the final velocity of an object when the beginning velocity, acceleration and time are known.

$$v_f = v_0 + at$$

For example, a car is moving at 10 meters per second on the freeway and accelerates by 2 m/s2 for the next 3 seconds. How fast is the car now going? In this question V0 is 12 mph, acceleration is 2 m/s2, and time is 3 seconds. Therefore the problem would be solved as follows:

$$v_f = 12 + (2)(3) = 18 \, m/s$$

The third kinematic equation can be used to solve for the final velocity in situations which only the initial velocity, acceleration, and distance traveled are known, and the time traveled remains unknown.

$$v_f^2 = v_i^2 + 2ad$$

For example, if a person were to run at a constant acceleration of 1.5 m/s2 for a distance of 50 meters, starting from a stopped position, their final speed could be calculated in the following manner:

$$v_f = \sqrt{(0)^2 + 2(1.5)(50)} = 12.2 \, m/s$$

Although these equations and concepts are simple, they are essential building blocks of further understanding physics. These equations are all used to describe the motion of an object. These principles of these equations are based off of the work of Sir Isaac Newton. Newton is one of the most well-known physicist and mathematicians because of his extensive work in the study of motion and forces. Rather than simply describing motion, Newton developed three laws of motion that explain the forces underlying the motions that the kinematic equations (above) describe.

Newton's First Law

Newton's First Law of Motion is also known as the Law of Inertia. This law states that an object in motion will stay in motion unless another force acts upon it. In other words, objects have inertia – a resistance to a change in their velocity or acceleration (motion). Prior to Newton's time, the prevailing belief was that the natural state for an object to be in was at rest. Unless a force continues to act on an object it will remain at or return to rest. Inertia claims the opposite of this. Based on this principle an object at rest will stay at rest, and an object in motion will stay in motion. The reason that things come to a stop on Earth is because of the opposing force of friction. Without friction, objects would remain in motion.

All motion is caused by an imbalance of forces. When all of the forces that are acting on an object are in balance, then the object is said to be at equilibrium. For example, consider a textbook that is sitting on a table. The force of gravity is pushing down on the book. The table offers a supporting force that pushes in equal magnitude upward. If the force of gravity were greater than the supporting force of the table, then the table would collapse and the book would fall to the ground. Alternatively, if the supporting force of the table were greater than the force of gravity, then the book would rise off of the table. Because the two forces are equal, the result is that the book remains motionless in equilibrium.

Another way to describe the term equilibrium is to say that the Net Force acting on an object is zero. The net force is overall force that is acting on an object once all forces have been taken into consideration. Forces are summed in each direction (up, down, and side to side) to determine what the net effect of the forces will be. If an object is in equilibrium, then it will always be zero.

Newton's Second Law

Newton's Second Law of Motion describes the behavior of objects for which the net force is not zero. According to Newton, the resulting motion, or acceleration, of an object is proportional to both the force acting on that object, and the mass of the object. It is described by the equation $F=ma$.

In this equation F refers to the net force. Force is measured in units named after Sir Isaac Newton. They are called Newtons (N). A Newton is the amount of force required to accelerate 1 kilogram at 1 m/s^2.

This is arguably the most important of Newton's three laws of motion because it allows for a practical, mathematical application of force. Based on this equation the net force can be used to analyze how an object will respond to a force. There are countless forces that can act on an object. The most common forces are listed in the following table.

Force	Description
Gravity	The force with which an object is being pulled towards the ground
Friction	A resistive force that occurs when two objects rub against each other
Normal Force	The supportive force that an object exerts when it is pushed against, such as a table with something set on it, or a wall with something leaning against it

Applied Force	A general term for any force that is being consciously exerted on an object by a person or other object
Tension	The force exerted by a string or wire that is being pulled tight
Spring Force	The resistive force exerted by a spring that is compressed or extended

Typically a tool called a force diagram is used to display the forces that are being exerted on an object so that they can be analyzed further. A force diagram is a simple sketch that shows the object in question, and the forces that are being exerted on it. Force diagrams can include as much information as is known about the situation, including the mass of various objects, and the magnitude of forces in question. For example, the following force diagram describes a box that is sitting on a table.

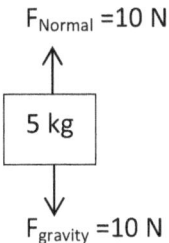

As you can see from the diagram, there is a 10 N normal force and 10 N gravitational force acting on the 5 kg box. The two forces combine with the result being a net force of zero.

Therefore, the box will not accelerate. However, if someone were to come past and push the box across the table, the diagram may look as follows:

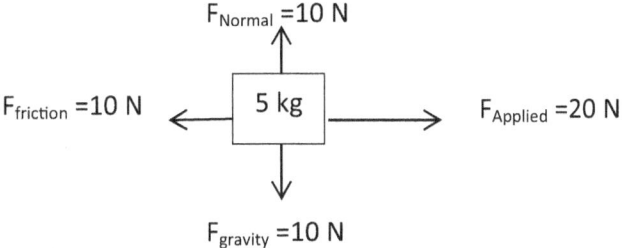

Here the sum of the vertical forces is still a net zero. However, the new applied force of 20 N countered with the opposing frictional forces of 10 N will result in a net force of 10 N to the right. This means that the box will accelerate to the right for as long as the force is applied. Using Newton's equation, we can even determine what the acceleration of the box will be:

$$F = ma$$
$$10 = 5(a)$$
$$a = 2\,m/s^2$$

Knowing the acceleration, the kinematic equations from earlier in the section can now be used to determine even further information about the velocity and position of the box over time. For example, given that a net force of 3 N acts on a 2 kg object, it is possible to determine its position and velocity over a given period of time. If the given time is 5 seconds, the first step is to determine acceleration using Newton's Second Law:

$$F = ma$$
$$3 = 2(a)$$
$$a = 1.5\,m/s^2$$

Now the acceleration of 1.5 m/s2 can be used to determine the distance traveled and the velocity at 5 seconds:

$$v = v_0 + at$$
$$v = 0 + (1.5)(5) = 7.5\,m/s$$

$$d = v_0 t + \frac{1}{2}at^2$$
$$d = 0(5) + \frac{1}{2}(1.5)(5)^2 = 18.75\,m$$

Newton's Third Law

Newton's third and final law has to do with actions and reactions. It states that for every action (or force) there is an equal and opposite reaction. Essentially this means that every interaction between two objects there are equal forces acting in opposite directions upon each object. For example, consider a collision between two cars. In this scenario, imagine that Car A is moving with a force of 500 N, and collides into a motionless Car B. Car A pushes Car B several feet to the left, and then stops.

Through the collision, Car A will have exerted 500 N of applied force on Car B. This sudden application of force is what accelerated Car B and caused it to move several feet. The force most likely caused a fair amount of damage to the car as well. However, according to Newton's Third Law, the collision will also result in an equal and opposite reaction force of 500 N being applied by Car B against Car A. That reactionary force is what brings Car A to a stop, and takes the form of friction and normal force that are exerted when Car A runs into a motionless object (Car B).

Another example of Newton's Third Law is a canoe. A canoe is propelled forward by the use of oars. When an oar is run through the water, the force of it pushes water backwards. In line with Newton's Third Law this requires that an equal and opposite force be present and that is what pushes the canoe forward through the water.

Newton's three laws revolutionized scientific thought. The principles that they contain are still some of the most important and widely used today. Newton didn't just seek to use his laws to describe motion on the planet Earth, however. He also sought to apply these principles to gravitation and planetary motion on a large scale. In doing so, he further studied and proved three laws of planetary motion that had been developed by Johannes Kepler. Kepler had been a student of famous astronomer Tycho Brahe. After Brahe's death, Kepler obtained his vast astronomical data. By studying this data, particularly related to the planet Mars, Kepler was able to make significant breakthroughs regarding the structure of the solar system, and motions of the planets.

Kepler's First Law

Kepler's first law states that the planets orbit about the Sun in elliptical orbits, with the Sun at one foci. This was a truly revolutionary idea – so much so that even Kepler was unsettled by it. Astronomers had always held that the planets must orbit in perfectly circular patterns. This belief was used in the earliest solar system models, and was so ingrained that even Copernicus didn't question it when he proposed the heliocentric model. Eventually, though, Kepler was led to the inevitable conclusion that only elliptical orbits would explain the detailed observations that Brahe had made. For most of the planets in this solar system, the orbits are only slightly elliptical.

Kepler's Second Law

Kepler's second law is also known as the law of equal areas. This law describes the speed with which a planet orbits. Because of the elliptical nature of planetary orbits, the speed at which the planets are orbiting changes constantly. Kepler observed that the speed of orbit will increase as the planet moves closer to the Sun, and then it will decrease as the planet moves away. Based on his observations, Kepler was able to determine that the amount of area passed by the planet would be the same over any equal period of time.

In other words, imagine that an imaginary line were drawn from any given planet to the Sun. The amount of area swept out by that line will be the same for any two equal periods of time. Therefore, the planet will move faster when it is closer to the Sun (and therefore sweeps out less proportional area when it moves) and slower when it is farther away (and will sweep proportionally more area for less movement). This is shown in the diagram below.

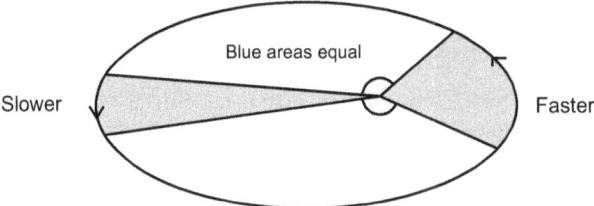

Each of the shaded sections represents the same amount of time passed. Although the actual motion and distance covered by the planet are quite different, the shaded areas will be equal.

Kepler's Third Law

Kepler's third law is often referred to as the law of harmonies. Kepler believed that there was a melodic harmony to the way that the universe worked, and he was a deeply spiritual man. The discovery of this law was further evidence to him of the harmony of the Universe. Kepler's third law describes the relationship between a planet's period of orbit and its distance to the Sun. The significance of Kepler's discovery was not known to him or his colleagues. It was later when Newton examined Kepler's work that the proportion became the foundation for Newton's understanding of gravity, and his development of the Law of Universal Gravitation.

Kepler's third law states that the square of the period (or time to make a complete orbit) is proportional to the cube of the average distance from the Sun. In other words, where T is the period of a planet's orbit, and R is the average distance from the Sun.

GRAVITY

Gravity is one of the most clearly visible forces in the world. It is a constant presence that affects every action from building construction, to walking, to standing up in the morning. Yet, as intuitive as the concept of gravity may seem today, there was very little understood about it before Sir Isaac Newton. Although Kepler developed three laws of planetary motion that governed the movements of planets throughout the solar system, even he did not have a satisfactory answer for why the planets behaved the way that they did, or what kept them in that motion. Some people believed that some sort of magnetic field compelled the planets to keep on their course.

Newton's breakthrough came when he realized that the forces that pulled objects on Earth's surface downward were likely the same forces that governed the movement of the planets also. He knew that the elliptical orbital pattern followed by planets couldn't simply be random – that would defy the law of inertia which requires a continued straight path in the absence of any additional forces. Furthermore, the reason that the Moon would orbit the Earth rather than the Sun was also anomalous.

Following this line of reasoning, Newton considered what would happen if a cannonball were shot from a very high cliff. It would travel for some distance and then begin to fall to the Earth as gravity forced it to accelerate downward. If the cannon were shot again from the same position and with even more force, then logically the same thing would happen, but with the cannonball traveling farther the second time. Newton theorized that there would be some amount of force with which the cannonball could be launched that would allow it to travel parallel to the Earth – being pulled down towards the Earth at the same rate that the Earth's surface curved underneath it. The cannonball would be in orbit.

This understanding was applied to the orbit of the Moon. It was being affected by gravity, but in such a way that it never fell all the way to the Earth. With this realization, all that was left was to find a way to mathematically describe gravity, and it's affects in the physical world.

LAW OF UNIVERSAL GRAVITATION

Newton is not simply famous for having theorized about the concept of gravity. Rather, he is famous because he described the universality of gravity. In other words, that it not only applied to Earth, but that the laws of gravity apply throughout the solar system and in the same ways that they do on Earth. Based on his knowledge of the Moon, Newton was able to determine that the Moon was 60 times farther from the center of the Earth than an object on the surface of the Earth. He used this to prove that the force of gravity is inversely proportional to distance from the center of the Earth.

This is only a piece of the puzzle, however. The full answer is known as the Law of Universal Gravitation. Based on his second law, Newton argued that the force of gravity was proportional to the mass of an object and inversely proportional to the distance. His next task was to determine the universal constant that would make the proportion true. In other words, Newton's Law of Universal Gravitation can be described as follows:

$$F_{grav} = \frac{G \cdot m_1 \cdot m_2}{d^2}$$

Where m1 and m2 are the masses of the two objects, respectively, and d is the distance between the centers of the two objects. G represents the universal constant by which gravity can be determined, known as the constant of gravitation.

The actual value of this constant G was not discovered for nearly one hundred years. It was discovered by Lord Henry Cavendish. Although it has gotten slightly more accurate with time, Cavendish was remarkably close. The value of G that is used today is 6.67x10-11. It's an incredibly small number which explains why gravity is typically only noticeable for objects with an enormous mass (such as the Earth). This value can be used in calculations to determine the force of the gravitational pull that exists between any two objects in the universe with known mass and distance apart.

ENERGY

Force is an important concept used to understand and describe the motion of objects, but it is not the only measure that scientists use. Two other related concepts are those of work and energy. Work is done whenever a force is used to transfer energy. Another description of work is that it occurs when a force causes displacement (or change in position) of an object. Work is calculated using the formula Work = Force x Displacement. For example, imagine that a force of 5 N is applied to a box and moves it for 10 meters. The work done would be calculated as W= (5)(10) = 50 J. The "J" stands for Joules, the unit that work is measured in.

One factor that complicates the calculation for Work is when a force is applied in a direction that is not parallel to the direction of motion. Remember that work is only done if the force causes a displacement to the object. For example, imagine that rather than pushing the box straight to the side in the previous example, the box were pushed at a downward angle of 60 degrees. In this case, trigonometry would need to be used to break the force into horizontal and vertical components. Only the vertical component of the force would be used in the calculation of the work.

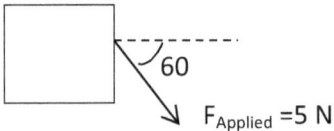

In this situation, the horizontal component of the force would be calculated by multiplying the total force applied, 5 N, by the cosine of 60 degrees to determine the vertical component:

(5 N)cos(60)= 2.5 N

Therefore, when the force is applied at this angle, the work done is

Work = Force x Displacement = 2.5 N x 10 meters = 25 J

These calculations can also be further used along with the kinematic equations and Newton's laws to further analyze the motion of the box, such as by determining the acceleration of the box, or the amount of time it would have taken to move it this distance. Hence, all of the mathematic descriptions of motion work in harmony. This pattern continues with the principles of energy.

Energy is defined as the ability of an object to do work (in other words, to be moved or transformed by a force). Energy is measured in two primary forms: mechanical energy and chemical energy. Chemical energy is a form of internal energy that is released due to chemical reactions. For example, the chemical reactions that occur when an individual digests food and transforms it into energy, or when something is burned and heat is generated. Although this form of energy is important, mechanical energy is typically more relevant in the study of motion.

Mechanical energy is used to describe external forms of energy. When people refer to energy this is typically what they are referring to. One way to think about mechanical energy is as the result of work having been done. For example, if work is done on an object, meaning that a force acts on an object such that it sets it in motion, the result is that the object will have gained mechanical energy. Similarly, if work is done on an object that prevents its motion (such as a car hitting a wall), then mechanical energy has been lost. Both situations describe external forces (a wall or an applied force) changing the energy of an object. Energy and work are closely connected. When work is done, energy has been transferred. The most common forms of mechanical energy are kinetic energy and potential energy. Each form of energy is used to describe a different capacity in which work can be performed, and the total mechanical energy is the sum of the two.

The first form of mechanical energy, kinetic energy, describes the energy of an object in motion. Kinetic energy can be calculated using the following equation:

$$E_K = \frac{1}{2}mv^2$$

In other words, the kinetic energy of an object is proportional to its velocity squared. This clearly demonstrates how work can be seen as a transfer of energy. If a net force acts upon an object, by definition it will change the velocity of the object. This will either increase or decrease the amount of kinetic energy present. Therefore, the energy will have been transferred to or taken from the object. This is the definition of work.

For example, imagine a 2 kg box that is sliding along the ground at a speed of 2 m/s. Over time the force of friction causes that box to slide to a stop. The work done on the box can be calculated as follows:

Work = Change in Energy

$$Work = \frac{1}{2}mv_f^2 - \frac{1}{2}mv_0^2$$

$$Work = \frac{1}{2}(2)(0)_f^2 - \frac{1}{2}(2)(2)_0^2 = -2J$$

Because energy was removed from the box (i.e., it stopped) the amount of work is negative. If energy is added to an object (e.g., if its velocity were to increase) then the amount of work done is positive.

The second form of mechanical energy is potential energy. Potential energy is the term used to describe energy that has been stored – typically as a result of position. There are two common forms of potential energy: gravitational potential energy and elastic potential energy.

Gravitational potential energy is present when objects are positioned above the ground. This gives the force of gravity an opportunity to do work on the object. When the object is above the ground, for example a bird flying through the air, the force of gravity will be acting on that object. When the object falls (or in the case of the bird, dives down), then work will have been done on the object because a force will have resulted in a change in movement. Gravitational potential energy is calculated proportional to mass, height, and the acceleration of gravity (which is a constant 9.8 m/s2). In other words:

$$E_{Potential} = m \cdot g \cdot h$$

For example, imagine that a 10 kg box is sitting on the edge of a table 1 meter above the ground. The potential energy of that box would be 98 J, calculated as follows:

$$E_{Potential} = (10kg)(9.8m/s^2)(1m) = 98J$$

The other form of potential energy is elastic potential energy. Whereas gravitational potential energy describes energy that is stored as a result of height, elastic potential energy is energy stored due to tension or elasticity in a spring or rope or other object. For example, when a spring becomes coiled then there is a potential for it to be released and exert a force on another object. This essentially stores energy for an object that may be moved by that force. For example, if a box is put in place at the end of the spring, and the spring is compressed, then the box has stored elastic potential energy.

Elastic potential energy can be calculated using the following equation:

$$E_{spring} = \frac{1}{2}kx^2$$

Where x is the amount that the spring is compressed, and k is the spring constant. The spring constant is different for each spring. It describes the amount of elasticity within the spring. For example, a very stiff spring that is difficult to compress or extent will have a higher value for k. A spring that stretches easily will have a very low value for k.

The various forms of energy – gravitational, elastic, and kinetic – are highly related to each other. An object shifts between different types of energy whenever a force is exerted upon it. For example, an object with gravitational potential energy falls and gains kinetic energy. Or, an object with elastic potential energy is set in motion and gains kinetic energy when the spring is released. This observation has led to the development of three Laws of Thermodynamics which describe the foundational governing principles of energy (thermodynamics is the study of energy).

First Law of Thermodynamics

The first law of Thermodynamics is also known as the Law of Conservation of Energy. This law states that energy cannot be created or destroyed – only transformed. In essence, we know that the total amount of energy in the universe is constant.

For example, a large object on top of a shelf has gravitational potential energy. This form of energy is proportional to height, so when the object falls the gravitational potential energy decreases. However, this energy is not lost. The act of falling has set the object in motion and the gravitational potential energy is simply transformed into kinetic energy. As the object reaches the floor, it will have a kinetic energy equal to the initial amount of gravitational potential energy – the energy is conserved.

The example becomes slightly more confusing once the object hits the ground. At this point it will have no kinetic energy (because it is no longer in motion) and no gravitational potential energy (because it is no longer elevated above the floor). The energy seems to have been destroyed. This discrepancy is explained by the Second Law of Thermodynamics.

Second Law of Thermodynamics

The Second Law of Thermodynamics is known as the Law of Entropy, or the Law of Increasing Disorder. Entropy is essentially the amount of disorder within a system. According to the Second Law of Thermodynamics the amount of entropy, or disorder, within a system will increase when chemical reactions take place. What this means is that chemical reactions convert energy from a useful form to an unusable form. For example, when food is digested and used to power a human body, it is not lost once used, but it can no longer be accessed for practical use.

In the example above, what happens when the object hits the ground is that the energy dissipates, or spreads out into the surrounding area. The force with which it hits the ground will cause the molecules and atoms to vibrate, imperceptibly heating the area. This is the chemical reaction in which the energy is transformed into an inaccessible state. Therefore, the total entropy of the system will have increased, consistent with the Second Law of Thermodynamics. Heating is the primary way in which energy is dissipated.

Any time a reaction occurs, there is some measure of energy that is dissipated. This is why the concept of a perpetual motion machine (a machine which can indefinitely power itself) is not possible. At some point, the machine will need an added measure of energy because of energy that is dissipated as entropy.

Another example of this concept is a hot frying pan. When a pan is put on a stove the heat energy will transfer from the hot coils to the metal of the pan. When the pan is then removed from the stove the pan will eventually cool. Based on the law of conservation of energy this is an anomaly. The heat energy should remain constant, requiring the pan to remain at the same temperature. However, the natural tendency of the energy is to dissipate, or disperse itself into its surroundings. This is entropy. The heat from the pan will dissipate to the surface it's placed on and into the air, and then from those places it will continue to spread further. At this point, that energy cannot be reclaimed. As a result the entropy, or disorder, of the system will have increased.

RELATIVITY

Thus far, all of the principles of Newtonian physics – those relating to force, motion, and energy – have assumed certain absolutes to exist. Specifically time, space, and mass are all assumed to have absolute boundaries. However, when relative motion is brought into the situation the concepts become much less absolute. For example, consider two cars that are moving towards each other at 50 miles an hour. To the observer in one car, it appears as if the oncoming car is moving at 100 miles an hour, whereas to an outside observer it appears as if the car is moving only 50 miles an hour. This is a simple example of relativity that can be overcome by simply defining an appropriate frame of reference. However, as scientists in the 19th century began testing more extreme situations such as the nature of light, it quickly became clear that there was more to be understood in the field of relative motion.

The most famous theorist in the field of relativity is Albert Einstein. Einstein developed a theory of relativity that reconciled Newtonian concepts with the extreme situations observed through the study of light. His theory begins with the assertion that the laws of physics are applicable in all frames of reference. For example, an experiment done in a stationary classroom should yield the same results if it is performed in a bus (assuming that the bus is moving is in a straight path at a constant velocity). This is because the laws will apply the same regardless of what frame of reference the experiment is performed in.

This concept is true because of the second assertion of Einstein's theories – that light travels at a constant speed regardless of an object's motion. This fact is what actually sparked Einstein's research and led him to generate the Special Theory of Relativity. It was proven with the Michaelson-Morley experiment. In the experiment Michelson and Morley attempted to measure the speed of the Earth relative to the speed of light. They did this by measuring the speed of light parallel to the Earth's movement and perpendicular to the Earth's movement. The results were surprising: Michelson and Morley discovered the speed of light to be the same in all directions. This proved that the speed of light was constant regardless of frame of reference, and seemed to defy the known laws of physics. Einstein built on their experiment to show that it was not the laws that were incorrect, but that certain concepts considered to be absolute – mass, length, time, and energy – were actually relative to the particular frame of motion.

The first to concepts that the Special Theory of Relativity shows to be relative are those of time and space. The Michelson-Morley experiment showed that the speed (or velocity) of light was constant regardless of direction- approximately 300 million meters per second. Because speed is determined as distance divided by time either time or distance must be relative. The relativity of space is explained by length contraction, and the relativity of time is explained with the concept of time dilation.

Length contraction simply refers to the fact that the faster an object moves, the more its length contracts. Moving at normal speeds this length contraction is imperceptible – which is why it never factored in to Newtonian physics. However, as an object approaches the speed of light its length contracts more and more until it approaches zero. This is why Einstein stated that the speed of light is the upper boundary for the speed at which an object can travel. No object with mass can travel at the speed of light or else its mass would disappear as its length contracted. Therefore, only massless light particles called photons can move at that speed.

Time dilation explains the skewing of time as frames of reference change. This can be explained with the concept of a photon clock. Imagine what would happen if a photon were to be timed as it bounced between two mirrors. The photon would reflect back and forth between the two mirrors at a constant speed – the speed of light. This is shown in the top figure.

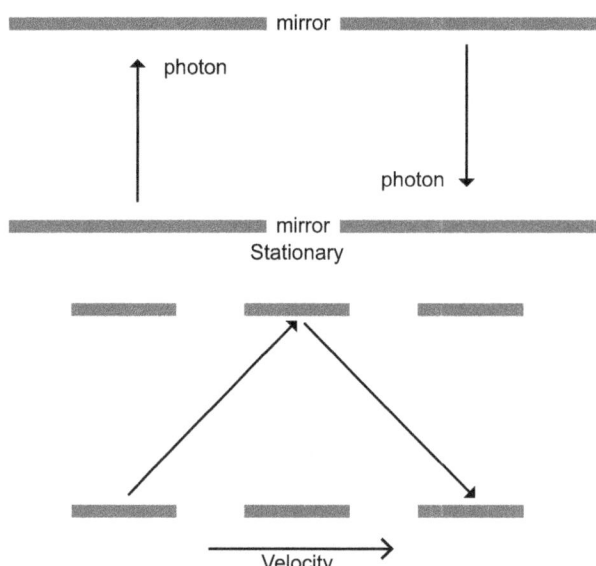

Now imagine that the mirrors were placed on a space shuttle and launched into space. To an observer the motion of the photon would remain exactly as it had before. However, if another person were watching from a different stationary location, say a space station, the motion would appear as it does in the bottom figure. Rather than simply moving up and down, the movement of the space shuttle would cause the photon to appear to move at a diagonal. This causes time dilation, or stretching and contracting of time. Remember that the speed of light is constant regardless of the frame of reference of the observer, so both individuals would see the photon particle moving at the same speed. However, the second observer sees the same photon particle moving a greater distance at that speed. In order for the particle to maintain the same speed over a greater distance, time itself must alter and increase in speed. What Einstein discovered was that the faster an object moves, the more time dilates, or skews. Faster moving objects experience time moving more slowly. The closer an object moves to the speed of light, the more slowly time passes.

The implications of the Special Theory of Relativity extend even further beyond space and time. The theory also extends to measures that are affected by changes in velocity – including momentum (which is measured as mass x velocity) and energy (remember that kinetic energy is a function of velocity). The link that Einstein discovered to explain the variations in these measures as a result of changing time frames is known as mass-energy equivalence.

The concept of mass-energy equivalence is described by Einstein's famous equation: $E=mc^2$. In the equation E represents energy, m represents mass, and c represents the speed of light. Essentially the equation shows that mass and energy are directly related to each other at a ratio equal to the speed of light squared. The full significance of this discovery was not fully appreciated until much later. This relationship is what allows nuclear fusion and nuclear fission.

To better understand the significance of mass-energy equivalence, consider the processes of nuclear fusion. Nuclear fusion is now known to be the process that powers the Sun – and therefore makes all life on Earth possible. Nuclear fusion is the process of fusing, or combining, two atoms and converting them into an entirely new atom. In the case of the Sun hydrogen atoms are fused with the resulting element being helium. This is possible because as two hydrogen atoms undergo intense collision, one of the protons converts to a neutron. However, the total resulting mass of the particles is decreased in the process. Remember that $E=mc^2$. Therefore, as the total mass of the particles decreases, there is an equivalent release of energy. Although it takes a great amount of energy to force the two repelling protons together, the release of energy when it occurs is even greater, and is the reason for the brightness and heat released by the Sun. Hundreds of millions of atoms are fused every second.

Celestial Systems

EARTH AND THE SKY

HOW OXYGEN ENTERED THE EARTH'S ATMOSPHERE

Current estimates put the formation of the Earth approximately 4.5 billion years ago. The process began with the formation of the Sun at the center of the solar system. After the Sun began to form at the center of a great nebulous cloud, its large gravitational pull began to flatten the cloud of gasses and debris into a flat disc, and more dense sections began to form themselves into planets. Collisions occurring between moving asteroids and planetoids grew in mass and gravitational pull, with one very large collision having the result of tilting the axis of the Earth's rotation, and freeing a large portion of lighter material that remained in orbit as the Moon. The ultimate result of various collisions and cosmic events is the Earth, and solar system, as it exists today.

The early Earth bore little resemblance to the one that exists today, however. It began as a molten mass that eventually cooled, allowing for the presence of liquid water. Volcanic activity and gasses remaining from the Earth's original formation resulted in an atmosphere that would have been toxic to life.

This leads to the question, how did Earth's atmosphere come to be composed of nearly 25% oxygen? The breathable form of oxygen that is found so abundantly in Earth's atmosphere is actually fairly uncommon throughout the remainder of the universe. Although oxygen is the third most common element, it is also fairly reactive so finding it in its breathable state is rare. Oxygen did not begin to become an important element of the Earth's atmosphere until photosynthetic organisms came into existence 2 billion years ago – over a billion years after the Earth's initial formation.

These photosynthetic organisms are known as cyanobacteria – a type of blue-green algae. Cyanobacteria are essentially the precursors to the organelles known as chloroplasts that make photosynthesis possible in plants today. Although little is known about what caused these bacteria to emerge or how they were able to gain enough prominence to significantly alter the Earth atmosphere, it is clear that their development and ensuing oxygen production is what allowed further development of life.

Just as the Earth in its early formation was greatly influenced by cosmic events, it continues to be influenced by interactions with other bodies throughout the solar system and the universe. For example, views of the night sky fascinate and dazzle onlookers; star formations are used in navigation; the rotations of the Sun and Moon affect seasons, tides, and the measurement of time. The existence of Earth is inseparably connected with the universe, and so scientists continue to seek further understanding of the mechanisms and processes that govern it. But this first involves creating a system by which to classify and track the movements of celestial bodies, allowing further study of how the universe functions. The system used today is known as the celestial coordinate system.

CELESTIAL COORDINATE SYSTEM

The night sky stretches out in a vast expanse around the Earth. Although it's easy to see that the Earth is simply an insignificant planet on the outskirts of a small galaxy, when astronomers look at the night sky they identify stars based on their location relative to the Earth. For this reason the vast expanse of space is often referred to as the Celestial Sphere.

To understand the concept of the celestial sphere, picture the night sky as a massive rotating sphere for which Earth is at the center. The rotation of the Earth causes the appearance that the celestial sphere is rotating from East to West – mimicking the rotation of the Earth. Knowing this allows the relative positions of stars to be tracked and identified. This is the basic idea of the Celestial Sphere.

Based on the celestial sphere, the celestial coordinate system has been developed. This system is an extension of the concepts of latitude and longitude that are used to describe locations on the Earth's surface. With the celestial coordinate system the North Pole of the Earth is extended indefinitely as the North Celestial Pole. In the other direction the South Pole is extended through space as the South Celestial Pole. Just as the Earth rotates about its axis with the equator at the center, the Earth's equator is extended through space as the Celestial Equator. The term zenith is used to describe the point on the celestial sphere that is directly above the observer. These points become the reference points for the celestial coordinate system.

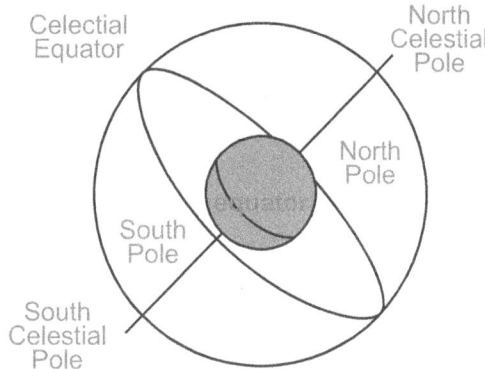

Further reference is made using measurements of Declination and Right Ascension. Declination is the equivalent in the celestial coordinate system of lines of latitude in the Earth's coordinate system. Using declination, the night sky is divided into segments totaling 180 degrees (because only half of the celestial sphere is visible at any given time). The declination is measured as the angle between the celestial equator and the object being studied. The angle is measured relative to the center of the Earth. Therefore, a celestial body which is located along the celestial equator (and is thus directly over the Earth's equator) will have a declination of zero.

Bodies that are located above the northern hemisphere, meaning those which are north of the equator, will have declinations ranging between zero and +90 degrees. For example, the star Polaris – more commonly known as the North Star – has a declination of 89 degrees, which is why it is commonly used to identify which direction is north. It lies almost exactly at the north celestial pole. Bodies that are located over the southern hemisphere have declinations between 0 and -90 degrees.

Another important measure is that of right ascension. Whereas declination is used as a measure of where a star appears in the night sky, right ascension is particularly helpful in describing when the star will appear. Right ascension is the spatial equivalent of longitude lines on Earth. Lines of right ascension run from the North Celestial Pole to the South Celestial Pole, and intersect the celestial equator perpendicularly. The 0 point for right ascension is determined as the point where the Sun crosses the equator on the vernal equinox.

Because right ascension is used to determine the time at which a star will be in a particular location, it is written in terms of hours and minutes. Each 24 hour period the measurement resets. Each hour is the equivalent of 15 degrees. So, for example, a star that were 2 hours right ascension could also be stated as 30 degrees right ascension. A star that is 5 hours and 35 minutes right ascension would be 83.75 degrees away from the starting point.

Historically the zero point for right ascension was measured near the constellation Aries. However, over a period of tens of thousands of years, the Earth "wobbles" slightly in on its axis. The result of this nearly imperceptible tilting is that now the vernal point of the Sun is closer to the constellation Pisces, giving it a right ascension near zero.

Based on a person's location on the Earth, their view of the sky will be very different. When a person stands at the equator and watches the night sky, the stars with declinations at or near 0 will appear to rise and set perpendicularly to the horizon, moving from east to west across the sky. Those stars which sit with declinations near the north celestial pole and south celestial pole will appear to move in half circles near the northern or southern horizons.

This all changes the further an observer is from the equator. For example, a person in Oregon would be near the 45th parallel. From this position the stars that are near -90 degrees declination (meaning those which surround the south celestial pole) will not be visible. They will not rise and set at all but will remain beneath the horizon. Furthermore, stars that from the equator appear to rise and set perpendicularly to the horizon will appear to rise and set at an angle as the observer moves further from that position.

Additionally, the stars with declinations near +90 degrees (meaning those which surround the north celestial pole) will be much more visible than they would be at the equator. Rather than moving in half circles near the horizon, these same stars would appear to move in circles around the Northern Celestial Pole. When stars appear to be circling, in cases such as this, they are called circumpolar. The closer an observer moves toward either the North Pole or the South Pole the more circumpolar stars they will observe. If an individual stands directly at the North Pole or the South Pole, all of the stars will appear circumpolar. At the North Pole no stars with declinations between 0 and -90 degrees are visible. At the South Pole no stars with declinations between 0 and +90 are visible.

THE SUN AND THE MOON ON THE CELESTIAL SPHERE

The majority of celestial bodies remain in fixed positions on the celestial sphere. This is not true for the two most apparent bodies to observers from Earth: the Moon and the Sun. Because the Moon rotates about the Earth and the Earth rotates about the Sun, each of these bodies experience slight changes throughout the course of the year in the positions relative to the Earth. This causes their position relative to the night sky to change.

In terms of the Sun's position relative to the Earth, the changes occur because the Earth is tilted on an axis of 23.5 degrees relative to the Sun. Because the Earth is not perpendicular to the Sun, the Sun does not have a declination of 0. This means that rather than rising and setting consistently over the equator, the Sun will rise and set at other locations on the horizon. However, as the Earth's rotation continues and the axis shifts in relation to the Sun, its declination and right ascension will change throughout the year. This causes position of the Sun to appear to move across the backdrop of the celestial sphere. The path that it takes is known as the ecliptic.

The ecliptic is also the origin of Zodiac symbols. As the Sun moves in its relative position on the celestial sphere, each month it is near a different constellation in the zodiac. From March to September the Sun appears north of the Celestial Equator, placing it near the constellations of Pisces, Aries, Taurus, Gemini, Cancer and Leo. From September to March the Sun appears south of the Celestial Equator, placing it near the constellations of Virgo, Libra, Scorpio, Sagittarius, Capricorn and Aquarius. Each year on the two equinoxes the Sun will line up perfectly over the equator. The point where this crossover occurs in the spring – the vernal equinox – is set as the standard for measuring right ascension.

The Moon follows the same ecliptic cycle that the Sun does, only it does so on a much smaller scale. Rather than taking a full year to work its way through the ecliptic path, the Moon makes this cycle each 29.5 days. Or, in other words, approximately every month as the Moon makes its full cycle around the Earth. As it goes through this cycle, the time at which the Moon rises and sets changes also (indicating that the ecliptic path affects both the declination and right ascension of the Moon).

EARTH AND THE MOON

PHASES OF THE MOON

Just as the Sun and Moon go through phases that determine their position on the celestial sphere, the Moon's changing position relative to the Sun and the Earth also results in phases that change its appearance throughout the course of each month. The Moon's light is a result of reflections from the Sun. Just as one side of the Earth is illuminated by the Sun at any given time, one half of the Moon is also illuminated at any given time. However, as the Moon circles around the Earth, different amounts of that illuminated portion are visible from Earth. Therefore, based on the Moon's position in its cycle more or less of the illuminated portion will be facing the Earth, despite the fact that the same amount of the Moon is illuminated by the Sun. This is the reason for the Moon's constantly changing appearance.

There are four main phases that the Moon cycles through each month – each phase lasting approximately one week. The four phases are known as the new Moon, first quarter, full Moon, and last quarter. At the new Moon, the Moon is positioned between the Earth and the Sun. As a result, the side of the Moon that is illuminated is facing completely away from the Earth, and the unilluminated side is facing towards it. Therefore, the Moon isn't visible at all because it is blocked out by the Sun's light.

At the quarter Moon the Moon has been to "grow." Rather than being between the Earth and the Sun, the Moon will have made one quarter of a rotation around the Earth and will be positioned to its side. This positioning means that half of the illuminated side of the Moon will be visible, and half of the unilluminated side will be visible. Therefore, at the first quarter, the Moon will appear as half of a circle. When the Moon is in between these first two phases – new Moon and first quarter – it is called a "waxing crescent." It is referred to as waxing because this means that it is growing, and it is referred to as a crescent because the shape of the Moon grows from barely a sliver into a half circle in a crescent pattern.

The third phase of the Moon is the full Moon. At the full Moon the Moon will have completed half of its circle around the Earth, meaning that it will have moved from being positioned between the Earth and the Sun to being positioned on the far side of the Earth. At this point the entire illuminated side of the Earth will visible to observers, and the Moon will appear as a full circle. As the Moon progresses from the first quarter phase to the full Moon phase it is called a waxing gibbous. At this stage rather than only seeing a crescent-like portion of the Moon (as in the waxing crescent phase) only a crescent-like portion of the Moon is missing. That portion becomes smaller and smaller as the Moon continues to grow (or "wax") to its fully visible full Moon state.

The fourth and final stage of the Moon is the last quarter stage. In this phase the Moon will have completed three-fourths of its circle around the Earth, placing it on the opposite side of the Earth as in the first quarter phase. Similarly to the first quarter phase, half of the illuminated portion of the Moon will be visible. The only difference is that it will be the opposite half as in the first quarter phase because the Moon is on the opposite site of the Earth. Between the full Moon and last quarter phases, the visible portion of the Moon will diminish each day. During this time it is called a waning gibbous. As with the waxing gibbous only a small crescent-shaped portion of the Moon appears to be missing. However, that "missing" portion grows, giving the appearance that the Moon is disappearing (or waning).

After progressing through each of these four cycles, the Moon will again return to its new Moon position – between the Earth and the Sun – and begin the cycle again. Between the last quarter and new Moon phases the Moon is described as a waning crescent.

Each of these phases of the Moon is pictured in the figure below. Remember, though, that these descriptions are simplified. The Moon does not progress through these stages in clear and dramatic ways. Rather, the change happens gradually throughout the course of a month. Each day the Moon will appear slightly different than it did the day before.

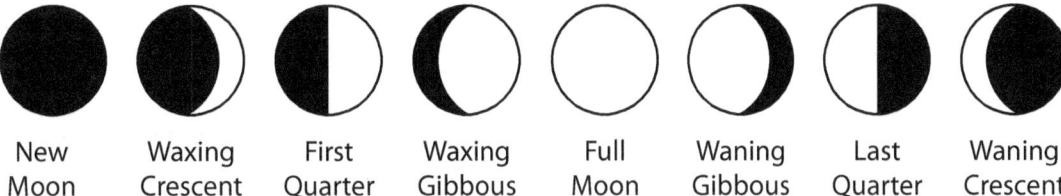

SOLAR AND LUNAR ECLIPSES

An eclipse occurs when part of one body is obscured or shadowed by another, blocking our view of it from Earth. There are two general types of eclipses: solar eclipses and lunar eclipses. The only times that they occur is during a new Moon or a full Moon respectively.

A solar eclipse can occur during a new Moon. It is caused by an alignment between the Earth, Sun and Moon that results in the Moon temporarily blocking out the Sun as it passes in front of it. Based on how well the three are aligned, and on an individual's relative viewing position on the Earth, the solar eclipse may appear partial, annular, or total. A total eclipse occurs when the Moon completely blocks all view of the Sun from Earth. An annular eclipse occurs when a small ring of the Sun is still visible around the Moon as it obscures the main body of the Sun. A partial eclipse occurs when the Moon and Sun are not perfectly aligned, and so only a portion of the Sun is obscured.

Why then, if solar eclipses and new Moons are both caused as a result of the Moon being in position between the Earth and the Sun, is there not a solar eclipse every month instead of simply a new Moon? The difference between the two can be explained by the ecliptic orbital patterns of the Moon and Sun. Remember that the Sun and Moon do not consistently orbit the Earth about the Celestial equator. Rather the delineation of their orbits changes throughout the month and year. As a result, the two rarely line up well enough to actually obscure one another. There can be anywhere from months to centuries between two solar eclipses because of this.

A lunar eclipse can occur during a full Moon. It is caused by an alignment between the Earth, Sun and Moon in which the Moon is placed on the opposite side of the Earth from the Sun. The positioning causes the Moon to pass through the Earth's shadow and block it from the Sun's light. Interestingly, rather than leaving the Moon darkened and preventing it from being viewed, the Moon will generally appear red or brown during a total lunar eclipse. This can be explained by the Earth's atmosphere. As the Sun's light hits the Earth, some of its rays are bent and refracted. The bluer shades are typically filtered out, but red light bends around the Earth and is essentially redirected towards the Moon. If not for the Earth's atmosphere, the Moon would be completely obscured during a lunar eclipse. However, unless the atmosphere is particularly thick and polluted (for example, shortly after a large volcano erupts) some light waves will curve around the Earth and fall on the Moon.

Just as with a solar eclipse, lunar eclipses do not occur every month because of the changing delineation of the Moon and Sun. Only when the Moon is positioned roughly equally across from the Sun will the eclipse occur rather than the typical full Moon.

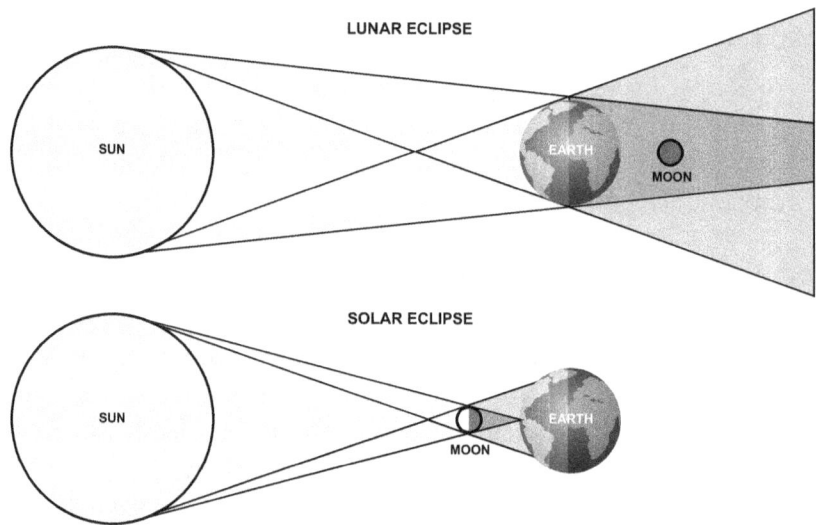

THE MOON AND TIDES

The Moon is the closest celestial body to the Earth. As a result, even though it is relatively small when compared with other planets throughout the solar system, its gravitational pull still has a great potential to influence events that occur on Earth. One excellent example of this fact can be seen in the tides.

The combined gravitational pulls of the Moon and the Sun as they act on the Earth cause the ocean to bulge in predictable ways. This phenomenon is known as a tide. The ocean levels are kept relatively constant around the Earth because of the delicate balance between gravitational forces within the Earth and centrifugal forces (which push outward from the Earth) caused by the Earth's rotation. Gravitational pulls from the Moon and, to a lesser degree, the Sun upset this balance. Depending on the alignment of the three planets at various times of day the ocean will be pull towards the Moon causing the water levels to increase at certain times of day, and then decrease at others.

Tides are not only created on the side of the Earth that is facing the Moon, however. Rather, the tidal bulges appear on opposite sides of the Earth at the same time. The second bulge can be attributed to the rotational force of the Earth. Remember that the water levels are kept as they are due to the balances between the rotational forces of the Earth and the pulls of gravity. This is why the excess gravitational pull of the Moon on the ocean waters is able to cause a bulge on one side of the Earth. Alternately, this results on a lessened gravitational force on the opposite side of the Earth which allows the rotational forces acting on the ocean to cause a bulge in the ocean waters to an equal extent. (If it helps, think of Newton's Third Law- for every action there is an equal and opposite reaction. This second tidal bulge acts equally and opposite to the bulge caused by the direct gravitational pull of the Moon.)

There are two primary classifications for tides – spring tides and neap tides. These two classifications of tides are connected to the phases of the Moon. Because both the Moon and the Sun have gravitational pulls on the Earth's oceans, when the two are in alignment, as would happen during a full Moon or a new Moon, then the two gravitational pulls combine and result in a tide that is more powerful than usual. This is known as a spring tide because of the increase in the waters "spring" towards the Moon.

Alternatively, when the Moon and the Sun are at a 90 degree angle relative to the Earth (such as occurs during a first quarter or last quarter Moon), then the gravitational pulls of the Moon and Sun are more distributed. Because the Moons gravitational pull is more powerful than that of the Earth the tidal pattern still continues, but it does so less dramatically than during a spring tide. These tides are known as neap tides.

Each month there are two neap tides – at the first quarter and last quarter Moon, and two spring tides – at the new Moon and full Moon. Additionally each day there are two periods of "high tide" (during each of the tidal bulges) and two periods of "low tide" (during the times in between tidal bulges). Tidal times vary throughout the day. Because the Moon's rotation varies slightly over the course of the month, the tides will similarly vary from day to day. Each day the tides occur approximately 50 minutes later than the day before.

TIDAL LOCKING

The impact of tidal forces is not reserved only to their impact on the Earth's oceans, however. These forces are in play all throughout the universe. They are also the reason for a phenomenon known as tidal locking (sometimes known as gravitational locking). The visible result of tidal locking between one body and another is that the tidally locked object will always present the same side to the body which it is locked to. For example, this is the case with the Earth and the Moon – the same side of the Moon is always facing towards the Earth.

The idea of a "dark side" of the Moon has fascinated mankind for centuries, although it is inaccurate. In reality the Sun illuminates different sides of the Moon on a regular basis – this is the reason that the Moon appears to go through different phases throughout the course of the month. What really occurs is that the rate of the Moon's rotation results the same side of the Moon consistently facing the Earth as it orbits around it.

When a planet is tidally locked to another its rate of rotation is the same as its orbit. In the Moon's case both is rotation about the Earth and its rotation about its own axis are slightly longer than 27 days. Because of this, as the Moon moves around the Earth – which should cause a different view its surface to be visible – its own rotation angles the same view of its surface back into view. This is also known by scientists as synchronous rotation.

The Moon was not always locked into synchronous rotation. Scientists believe that it was gradually pulled into it as a result of tidal forces exerted by the Earth. Just as the Moon's gravitational pull results in oceanic tides on the Earth's surface, the Earth's gravity causes bulges in the Moon's surface. These bulges are much less noticeable than the tides on Earth are because the Moon is composed of rock, which makes it much harder to manipulate. The bulges do exist, though.

This tidal bulging then affects the gravitational pull on the Moon from the Earth. Remember that gravitational force is proportional to distance. Therefore, the closer side of the Moon is pulled toward the Earth with greater force than the farther side is. As the Moon continues its rotation, the tidal bulges experience a slightly strong pull of gravity which over time results in a gradual slowing of its rotation until it has now reached the point of tidal locking.

There are several other bodies throughout the universe that similarly experience tidal locking. Eight of Jupiter's Moons – including Io and Europa – are tidally locked. Mars, Saturn, Uranus, and Neptune similarly have several tidally locked Moons. Pluto and one of its Moons – Charon – are tidally locked to each other.

TIME AND THE CALENDAR

DAYS, MONTHS, AND YEARS

Measurement of time is governed by the rotation of the Earth relative to other celestial bodies- primarily the Sun and the Moon. Days are measured as the amount of time that the Earth takes to revolve once about its own axis. Throughout history different cultures have measured the "end" of one day and "start" of another at different times in this rotation, but today the accepted standard is for the day to end and begin at 12:00 a.m. (midnight).

A year is measured as the amount of time that it takes for the Earth to complete one revolution about the Sun. This works out to be approximately 365.24 days. To account for the inexact amount of time, a year is measured as 365 days and each fifth year an extra "leap day" is inserted in February to keep the timing consistent.

Months are measured relative to the lunar cycle rather than the solar cycle as are days and years. Originally each lunar cycle (from new Moon to new Moon) was considered to be one month. However, just as the number of days in a year is not exact, neither is the number of lunar cycles in a year. There are approximately 12.4 lunar cycles in a year. Because of this, the calendar today includes 12 months with varying numbers of days (28-31).

SEASONS

A common misconception about seasons is that they are caused by the changing relative distance between the Earth and the Sun (because the Earth is locked in an elliptical cycle at some times of the year it is closer to the Sun than at others). However, the true cause for the changing seasons on Earth's surface is the tilt of the Earth's axis relative to the Sun.

The Earth is currently at a 23.5 degree tilt in its orbit about the Sun. The direction of the Earth's orbit is constant (meaning that it is always pointing towards the same relative position in the Universe). This causes different portions of the Earth to be closer to the Sun, and others to be farther from it, at different times of the year. This is why seasons become more exaggerated closer to the north and south poles, and less exaggerated around the equator.

This is also why the northern and southern hemispheres experience seasons at opposite times of the year. When the northern hemisphere is experiencing summer temperatures, the southern hemisphere will be experiencing winter temperatures (and vice versa). Interestingly, when the northern hemisphere is experiencing summer it is actually at its furthest actual distance from the Sun (remember that's its orbit is an elliptical shape).

EQUINOX AND SOLSTICE

The points at which seasons change are known as equinoxes and solstices. Solstices mark the points at which the Earth's position in its orbit is most dramatic - meaning that it is at either its furthest actual distance from the Sun (as it is during the Summer solstice in June) or its closest actual distance from the Sun (as it is during the Winter solstice in December). These two points mark the longest and shortest days of the year (in terms of Sunlight hours) and the beginning of the summer and winter seasons. The Winter solstice marks the shortest day of the year and the first day of winter. The Summer solstice marks the longest day of the year and the beginning of Summer).

The equinoxes, alternatively, are the points at which the Earth in midway between solstices. On these days the hours of daylight and the hours of Sunlight are exactly the same. The Autumnal equinox in September marks the beginning of autumn. The Vernal equinox in March marks the beginning of spring.

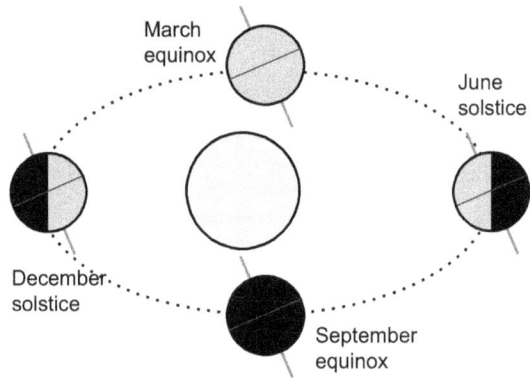

The Science of Light

THE ELECTROMAGNETIC SYSTEM

ELECTROMAGNETIC WAVES

There are two basic types of waves in the universe – mechanical waves and electromagnetic waves. Mechanical waves are waves that transfer energy through matter. For example, waves in water, the ground shaking during a natural disaster, or the movement of a jump rope are all examples of mechanical waves. Even sound is a form of mechanical wave. It requires the medium of air molecules to travel through. Otherwise there would be no such thing as sound – which is why in the vacuum of space there is no sound.

The other type of wave is electromagnetic waves. These waves do not require matter to travel through as mechanical waves do. Rather, they are composed of massless photons (little energy bundles) that move through space. Essentially, electromagnetic waves are light. But electromagnetic waves are not just the light that we can see with the naked eye. Rather, this classification includes an entire spectrum of light, the majority of which is invisible to the human. This is called the electromagnetic spectrum. Although each variety of light within the electromagnetic spectrum has distinct properties and scientific uses, each is essentially the same. The diagram below illustrates the basic properties of a wave.

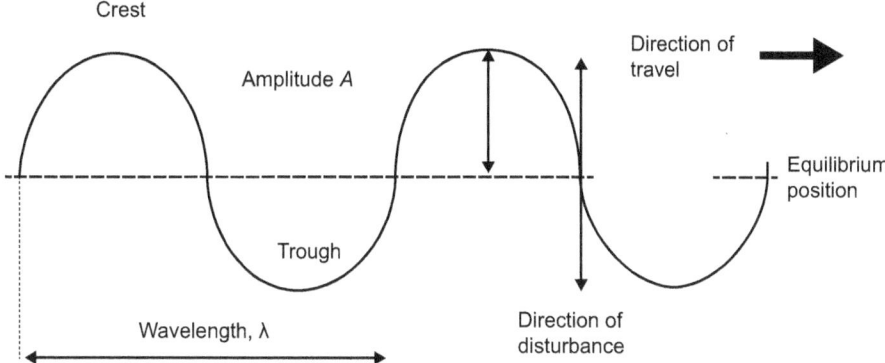

The amplitude of a wave is the height of the wave. Essentially it is a measure of the amount of disturbance caused by the wave. In light waves this is a function of how bright the light is. The greater the amplitude, the brighter the light will appear in comparison to other waves.

The wavelength of a wave is the length of one complete wave cycle. This can be measured from one crest (high point of the wave) to another, one trough (low point of the wave) to another, or from any other point along the wave, just as long as the measurement is taken from the location on the wave.

The wavelength of a wave is inversely proportional to the frequency. Frequency is the number of waves that will pass a specific point in one second. The frequency of light is measured in Hertz (Hz). One wave cycle per second is equivalent to 1 Hertz. This measure is named after Heinrich Hertz, a German physicist who first proved that radio waves are a form of electromagnetic wave. Because of the very rapid speed light waves travel at, their speed is generally referred to in Gigahertz (GHz). One GHz is approximately one billion wavelengths per second.

In more common terms, the speed of light is 300 million meters per second – approximately 670 million miles per hour. Because the universe is so vast, and because it is only observable through the analysis of light, the speed of light is commonly used in measures of distance in space. For example, the term "light second" is commonly used and is the description of how far light travels in one second – 300,000 kilometers or 186,000 miles. At this speed an object would circle the Earth around the equator 7.5 times in a single second.

Even this vast distance is not great enough for many astronomical measures. Light years are also a very commonly used measure of distance in space – the distance that light can travel in one year is 9.5 trillion kilometers (nearly 6 trillion miles).

Another common measure of distance in astronomy is that of a parsec. A parsec is a unit of measure based on the triangulation of a distance star relative to the positions of the Earth and the Sun. Parsec stands for the parallax of an arc second. Essentially, a measurement of the star's location is taken at two different points in time. As the Earth revolves around the Sun, the star in question will appear to have moved relative to the Earth. Trigonometry can then be used to draw an imaginary triangle between the Earth, Sun, and star. A parsec is the distance away that a star would be if the angle of its apparent movement were one arc second – 1/60th of a degree. A parsec is calculated as approximately 3.3 light years.

Waves that have a longer wavelength (and therefore lower frequency) are the lower-energy waves. Waves with a shorter wavelength (and therefore a higher frequency) are more high-energy waves. This is why different spectrums of light are used when observing different astronomical phenomenon – high energy stars and interactions give off certain types of light, whereas low energy interactions can only be observed by studying other types of light.

The way in which light interacts with an object can also be studied by astronomer's to determine more about that object. When light waves interact with an object they can be reflected, absorbed, diffracted, scattered, or refracted, depending on the specific properties of that object. Observing these interactions gives astronomer's clues about the composition and properties of various objects in space.

Reflection: Reflection occurs when light bounces off of a surface. For example, when light hits a mirror, nearly all of that light is reflected back towards the observer. Reflection is also the reason for color. When light hits an object, the majority of it is absorbed. The light that is reflected off its surface is what the observer will see when they look at that object. One way in which this principle of reflection has been used is in mapping objects such as the Moon. Lasers are shot at the surface of the Moon, and based on the amount of time it takes them to reflect, astronomers can determine how far they had to travel. Based on the relative depths of craters and heights of mountains can be mapped.

Absorption: Absorption occurs when, rather than being reflected, the energy from traveling light is absorbed into the object upon impact. This increased energy that has been absorbed causes the molecules to move faster and heat is emitted. This principle is the basis for infrared imaging. Infrared radiation is often absorbed and emitted as heat energy. Infrared cameras capture this heat information and display it.

Diffraction: Diffraction occurs when light bends and disperses around another object. This principle is both a blessing and a curse in the world of astronomy. Because light diffracts and distorts as it travels through space, it can make actual observation of objects more difficult. However, the principle is also used in a field called spectroscopy. Spectroscopy involved intentionally diffracting incoming light waves. The diffraction patterns can then be used to determine the chemical composition of stellar and interstellar matter.

Scattering: Light is said to have scattered when it collides with another object and as a result disperses in several different directions. Scattering is the reason that the sky appears blue. When light passes through the Earth's atmosphere the longer wavelengths (which represent the red end of the visible light spectrum) are able to continue passing through whereas shorter wavelengths (blue and violet) are broken up and are scattered.

Refraction: Refraction is similar to diffraction in that it involves light bending and changing direction. The difference between the two is that diffraction occurs when light bends around an object or an opening. Refraction occurs when light changes mediums. For example, when light passes through a prism it will fan out – such as how light refracting through raindrops creates a rainbow in the sky. Another example of this is that when a pencil is placed in water, it appears as if it is bent. Although the pencil remains just as straight, the light waves travel differently through water and air, so the pencil appears bent. The greater the wavelength of the light, the greater the amount of diffraction will be.

ELECTROMAGNETIC SPECTRUM

The electromagnetic spectrum is made up of seven different types of light waves. The lowest frequency of these is radio waves – traveling a few thousand Hz per second. In order of increasing frequency the other six waves are Microwaves, Infrared, Visible Light, Ultraviolet light, X-Rays, and Gamma Rays. Gamma Rays can have frequencies exceeding billions of GHz per second.

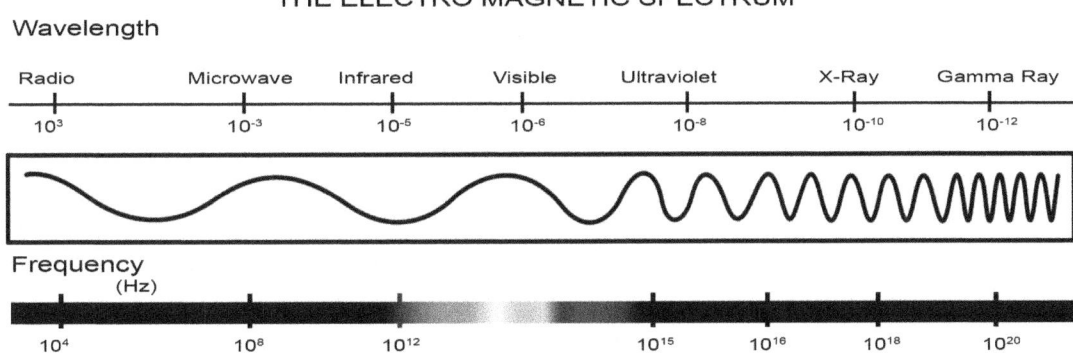

RADIO WAVES

Radio Waves are the largest, lowest energy forms of wave in the electromagnetic spectrum. They can range in size from about a foot all the way up to a football field in length. This requires radio telescopes to be very large in order to be able to receive transmissions from space. Even a 60 meter wide radio telescope may return an image no clearer than a simple optical telescope could. Often, radio telescopes are arranged in a series so that light can be collected and compiled from several telescopes for a greater picture.

On Earth these waves are used for audio transmission in radios, cars, and even cell phones. In space these waves are emitted from very distant regions of the universe. Especially because radio waves can easily travel through the dust clouds in space, allowing for images of areas that could not otherwise been seen using only visible light capabilities. The presence of radio waves can be used to learn more about quasars (quasar is short for quasi-stellar radio source), distant star-forming regions of the universe, and supernova remnants.

MICROWAVES

Everyone is familiar with the traditional food preparation use of microwaves, but few take the time to consider what is actually occurring within the microwave. Microwaves are actually a form of light (electromagnetic radiation). In the microwave, shorter waves around the length of a foot) are directed towards the food. Movement within the molecules causes transfers the energy from the microwaves into kinetic energy, with the ultimate result being heat dissipated from the friction as the molecules move.

Another important use of microwaves is in weather observance. Microwaves are categorized into several bands based on their frequency. Certain forms of microwaves have the distinction of being able to penetrate storms. These are used to capture images and determine temperature, wind speed, and other storm factors. For example, microwaves were used to gather images of Hurricane Katrina underneath the storm clouds. Microwave pulses can be sent out, and when they return wind speed and direction are determined based on the changes in energy level of the pulse.

Microwaves are also the form of Cosmic Background Radiation (CBR), a low-energy background radiation that fills the entire universe. This is thought to hold clues and evidence of the Big Bang Theory. The CBR was first discovered by Arno Penzias and Robert Wilson in the mid-1960's. While working with a low-noise antenna they picked up a background static. Originally they assumed it was a problem with the antenna itself, but after investigating further they knew it had to be a real signal.

The interesting thing about the signal that Penzias and Wilson identified was that it seemed to come from all directions with the same intensity, which made it highly unlikely that it was from any sort of local receiver. Eventually it was pointed out to them that such a background radiation had been predicted by scientists studying the Big Bang Theory. CBR supports this theory because only a cosmic event as encompassing as the Big Bang could have generated so much radiation at such consistent levels throughout the universe. The existence of CBR therefore supports the Big Bang Theory over the Steady-State Theory.

CBR is an important field of study because it would have been the first light to have originated after the Big Bang. Prior to the creation of this energy, the universe would have been so compacted, hot, and dense that light waves would have been unable to travel freely through it. Once the universe cooled to a point where molecules could begin forming light and energy would have been emitted. Over time that radiation has cooled to the state it is in today, the background microwave radiation that fills the universe. The more that is understood about it and its origins, the more scientists can determine about the early stages of the universe.

INFRARED RADIATION

The next form of light along the electromagnetic spectrum is infrared radiation. The primary way in which infrared radiation manifests is as heat – in fact, that is how it was discovered. In 1800 William Herschel was conducting an experiment to measure the temperatures of different colors of light within the visible spectrum. He discovered that temperature was lower on the blue side of the spectrum and higher on the red side of the spectrum. During the experiment Herschel noted that just outside the red end of the visible spectrum there was a notable temperature increase that followed the pattern of the light. Although it still couldn't be seen, infrared light had been discovered.

Infrared light is emitted by almost all objects in the universe in the form of heat. Some objects are hot enough that the heat manifests visibly, such as coals and fire. But even a person, animal, or block of ice will emit infrared light. This is advantageous to astronomers wishing to study objects that are too cool or distant to study within the visible light spectrum. The only problem is that unlike radio waves and microwaves, very few infrared waves are able to penetrate the Earth's atmosphere. This problem was solved by sending infrared telescopes into space.

VISIBLE LIGHT

The next shortest wavelength of light is visible light – so named because it encompasses the range of light that can be seen by the human eye. The majority of visible light that the average person on Earth will encounter emanates from the Sun, but visible light in present – if not easily viewed – throughout the universe. Visible light was the only method available to study the stars for centuries until other ranges of the electromagnetic spectrum were identified and studied. From the naked-eye observations of early astronomers such as Ptolemy, Aristotle, and Copernicus, through early telescopic observers such as Galileo, to today's far-reaching Hubble telescope, visible light observations are undoubtedly an invaluable method of studying the universe.

The unique characteristics of each color in the visible spectrum provide important information to astronomers. Each color within the visible spectrum is characteristic of a certain frequency of vibration. Red has the greatest wavelength – starting at around 750 nanometers (400 Hz) – and violet has the shortest wavelength – starting around 400 nanometers (700 Hz). The varying lengths of each color in the visible spectrum are the reason that rainbows exist and that prisms are able to break apart white light into individual colors. The amount of refraction that the light will experience is relative to its wavelength. Each color diffracts relative to its own wavelength, causing them all to refract at slightly different angles.

Although it may not be immediately apparent when looking at the night sky, not every star emanates the same exact color. Astronomers classify stars based on their relative brightness and color. Some stars shine bluer, whereas others have a more yellow or orange tinge. Still others appear red. Study of these subtle differences and the use of spectroscopy can allow astronomer's to determine the heat a star is burning with and its chemical composition.

ULTRAVIOLET LIGHT

Ultraviolet (UV) light is the range of electromagnetic waves that falls just beyond the violet end of the visible spectrum. Although ultraviolet rays are the popularly known source of Sunburns, very little of the Sun's ultraviolet rays are actually able to penetrate Earth's atmosphere – over 95% are absorbed before passing through the ozone layer of the Earth's atmosphere. These ultraviolet rays are found throughout the universe, particularly in regions of young star formation.

Ultraviolet rays don't penetrate through clouds, dust, or atmospheres well, so in order to view them, telescopes have been placed outside the Earth's atmosphere. Looking through the filter of ultraviolet light a majority of stars seem to disappear – they are too cool to emit such high frequency waves. Very old galaxies and very new, hot stars and galaxies are visible on the ultraviolet spectrum, however, making ultraviolet light observations a very effective way for astronomers to learn more about the changes that happen in a galaxy or star from its early stages, to its end.

The low penetration of ultraviolet light also makes it ideal for mapping interstellar clouds and dust. It is also used to study more about the Sun's atmosphere and surface conditions.

X-RAYS

Following ultraviolet rays in energy level are x-rays. X-rays have an incredibly small wavelength of .3-3 nanometers, which means that their wavelength is smaller than even some atoms. This indicates a very high energy wave. Because x-rays have such a high frequency, normal telescoping methods have to be adjusted to capture their light. While many optical telescopes use mirrors in order to capture, magnify and redirect light captured from stars, x-rays would continue straight through a normal mirror. Specially designed and angled mirrors must be used to study x-rays.

Another difficulty of studying x-rays is that a telescope must be set into orbit around the Earth in order to collect data about them. This is because x-rays cannot penetrate the Earth's thick atmosphere.

High energy waves such as x-rays are only emitted from hot astronomical bodies. Only bodies reaching millions of degrees Celsius emit light in this range. For example, the study of x-rays has been used in the discovery of black holes, and the study of supernovae. X-rays are also used to study the hottest regions of the Sun's corona – a thick, hot region of plasma that surrounds the Sun.

GAMMA RAYS

Gamma Rays are the highest frequency electromagnetic waves that have yet been discovered. They have such a small wavelength that they cannot be captured using telescopes and mirrors – the waves can easily pass through the atoms of any tool attempting to detect them. In order to observe these waves, instruments are designed to detect gamma rays by analyzing disruptions in the electrons of atoms as gamma rays pass through them.

Because gamma rays are so disruptive to the structure of atoms, they are very dangerous to living organisms. Luckily, gamma rays are completely blocked by the Earth's atmosphere. However, they are produced through nuclear reactions, and must be very carefully handled in order to be contained.

The hottest and most active elements of the universe are visible in the gamma ray spectrum. For example, black holes, high-speed collision, solar flares, and neutron stars. Each of these phenomena emits massive amounts of energy which are contained within gamma rays.

MEASUREMENT AND ANALYSIS OF LIGHT

SPECTROSCOPY

In addition to analyzing the various types of light that an object emits, astronomers use the study of spectral lines (spectroscopy) to discover more about astronomical bodies. The study of spectroscopy began with the study of visible light as it refracted through a prism. Sir Isaac Newton was the first to discover that light was really composed of several components (the various colors) that all refracted to different degrees.

As scientists continued to study this refraction process it was discovered that light from the Sun did not refract in a continuous pattern – there were dark lines across the color spectrum where light was not being refracted. Further study showed that in fact all elements refract with a different spectrum, and the study of these spectral signatures is known as spectroscopy. Initially the studies were done only in the visible light spectrum, but it is also possible to study the spectral signatures of objects in other wavelengths of light as well.

Today spectral lines are studied using instruments known as spectrometers. Spectrometers allow light to pass through a narrow slit and direct it towards a diffraction grating and then displays the resulting spectra. A diffraction grating is essentially a piece of glass with hundreds of thin lines etched into it that acts as a prism. The more lines that are etched into the diffraction grating, the more detailed the refraction pattern of the light (its spectra) will appear.

There are three general types of spectral signatures – continuous spectra, emission spectra, and absorption spectra. A continuous spectra appears as a completely, continuous rainbow pattern. In other words, all colors are refracted. Continuous spectra are typical of solid or liquid objects when heated – for example, people emit continuous spectra in the infrared range. Other objects that emit continuous spectra include incandescent light bulbs or heated coals. In astronomic terms, an object that emits a continuous spectrum is known as a blackbody. Blackbodies are objects that perfectly absorb all light. As the blackbody is heated it will emit electromagnetic waves in a continuous spectrum based on the temperature it is heated to.

Emission spectra are spectra that are essentially dark (no colors are refracted), but in which a few bright lines appear. Emission spectra are produced by heated, low-density gasses. In these gasses the molecules have a low incidence of collision (because of the low-density). As electrons within the atoms naturally move to lower energy levels, an electromagnetic wave will be emitted at a very specific frequency. This is what causes only specific wavelengths (colors) to appear on the spectral image.

Absorption spectra are nearly continuous spectra with certain frequencies missing from the spectrum (as was previously noted is the case with the Sun). An absorption spectra will occur when light in a continuous spectrum passes through a cooler gas. As the light passes through the gas energy will be absorbed at specific frequencies, causing holes in the spectrum. This is the case with the Sun because the Sun emits a continuous spectrum, but when the light passes through the Sun's atmosphere (a relatively cooler material than the Sun itself) certain frequencies of light are absorbed. Most stars will emit absorption spectra like the Sun does.

By studying the emission spectra of an object, astronomers are able to learn information about its chemical composition, heat, motion and size. This is because every element emits a unique spectral pattern. The strength of the pattern and combination of absorption lines reveal important clues about composition, heat, and size. Motion can be judged based on a principle known as the Doppler Effect.

DOPPLER EFFECT

The Doppler effect is a principle that applies to waves generated by objects in motion. A common example of this is a police siren. If you listen carefully, as the siren moves closer to you it will sound higher pitched, and as it moves away from you the pitch will get lower. This happens because as the siren moves towards you the sound waves will be compressed by the motion of the car. This results in a higher pitch because pitch is relative to the frequency of a sound wave. Then as the police car moves away the sound waves from the siren will be elongated, lowering their frequency and the pitch.

This same principle applies to light waves. When an astronomical object is moving towards the planet Earth, the light waves become compressed. This causes the spectral pattern of the light to be slightly shifted towards the blue (higher frequency) side of the color spectrum. Astronomers are able to calculate the speed and approximate direction that the object is moving in based on the amount of blue shift that an object exhibits.

The opposite is true for objects that are moving away from the Earth. As the object moves further away from the Earth the light waves that it emits will become elongated. The result is that the spectral pattern of the light will be slightly shifted towards the red (lower frequency) side of the color spectrum.

The vast majority of planets in the universe are red shifted, which causes astronomers to conclude that the universe is expanding. Furthermore, the further away a galaxy or star is, the greater its red shift is, meaning that the expansion of the universe is not constant – it is greater at the edges of the universe than in the middle.

Planetary Systems: Our Solar System and Others

CONTENTS OF OUR SOLAR SYSTEM

Our Solar System is composed of the Sun and all of the objects that are held in rotation around it – held it place by its vast gravitational pull. This includes the eight planets and their Moons, an asteroid belt, meteoroids and dwarf planets such as Pluto.

There are three general classifications of planets. The four closest to the Sun, and within the asteroid belt, are known as terrestrial planets because they are primarily composed of hard, rocky materials (such as the Earth). Beyond the orbits these four terrestrial planets are the gas giants – Jupiter and Saturn. These two planets share the characteristic of being largely formed of low density helium and hydrogen. The final two planets – Uranus and Neptune – are known as ice giants. They are so distant from the Sun in their orbits that they remain colder, and are formed of heavier, denser materials than the gas giants.

THE SUN

The Sun is the most massive object in our solar system, and its gravitational pull is what holds everything else within the solar system in place. In fact, the mass of the Sun accounts for 99% of the mass in the solar system. The Sun is a star much like those that fill the night sky. In fact, it is a relatively small star when compared with others throughout the universe, but its relative closeness to the Earth makes it seem larger. Without the light and heat radiated by the Sun, life on Earth would not be possible.

The Sun is estimated to be 4.5 billion years old. It is primarily composed of helium (around 8% of its mass) and hydrogen (around 90% of its mass). Throughout its lifetime, beginning with its lifetime, the Sun will progress through six different stages: Protostar, Main Sequence, Red Giant, Planetary Nebulae, White Dwarf, and Black Dwarf.

The protostar phase describes the time before the Sun was truly a star. At this point the matter that now composes the solar system was simply a large cloud of gas and dust. As the forces of pressure and gravity acted on the cloud (known as a nebula) the particles of gas and dust began fusing together and nuclear fusion began occurring. A star is considered to have been born once nuclear fusion begins. The Sun began fusing hydrogen 4.5 billion years ago, slowly contracting in size and increasing in temperature as it did so.

As gradual fusion of hydrogen into helium continued, the energy released by those reactions stopped the contraction of the Sun. This resulted in its progression to the relatively steady state it is currently it. This is the Main Sequence phase of the Sun. Today the Sun burns at approximately 27 million degrees Fahrenheit (15 million degrees Celsius).

The internal structure of the Sun in its current Main sequence phase can be described in six different layers. Active fusion occurs at its very dense, very hot core. Energy from the fusion reactions passes through the next layer of the Sun- the radiative zone - in the form of electromagnetic waves. The radiative zone is so named because the primary method of energy transfer in this zone is through radiation. Expanding outward from the radiative zone is the convection zone. In this region of the Sun's interior energy continues to pass outward through convection. Radiation from deeper down heats the radiative core, causing heated regions to push outward, cool, and fall back inwards. This creates a churning cycle of heating and cooling.

Beyond the convection zone is the photosphere. This is the lowest level of the Sun's atmosphere and is the portion that is seen when observing the Sun. Here the energy from the fusion reactions at the Sun's core is finally able to break free from the Sun in the form of photons (i.e. electromagnetic waves or light waves). Outside the photosphere is the chromosphere. This portion of the Sun's atmosphere extends for approximately 2500 kilometers and is visible as a red ring during solar eclipses (it is typically obscured from view by the much brighter photosphere). The outermost region of the Sun is the corona. The corona is a cloud of plasma that extends hundreds of thousands of miles around the Sun.

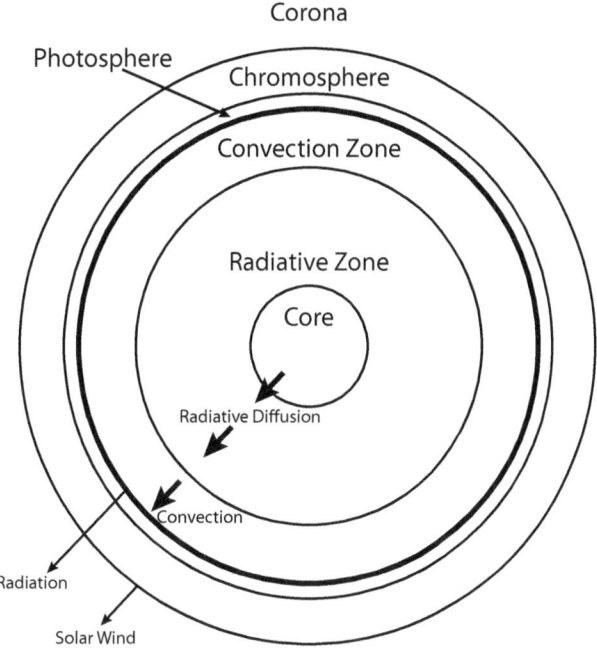

Some of the phenomena that are common on the surface of the Sun during its main sequence phase are flares, spicules, prominences, and sunspots.

Sunspots emerge within the photosphere. They are denser, cooler areas along the photosphere that have a very strong magnetic quality. Galileo first observed Sunspots in the early 1600s, and they have been tracked daily since the mid-1700s. Although they aren't completely understood, it has been discovered that sunspots seem to appear in regular cycles - peaking approximately once each decade.

The existence of highly magnetic Sunspots contributes to the generation of other solar phenomenon. Solar flares, for example, tend to emerge from areas around sunspots. A solar flare occurs when an explosion within the photosphere ejects great amounts of solar material into the air. The ejections are known as solar storms as they travel through space.

Spicules are similar solar flares, except that they occur from within the chromosphere. They appear as spikes and eject solar material into space at speeds of 50-70 miles per hour. Spicules tend to extinguish quickly – often after only a few minutes.

Lastly, prominences are clouds of solar material that have been pulled into the air (most likely by the Sun's magnetic fields). They appear as threadlike loops attached to the Sun, and can remain suspended in a relatively stable state sometimes for several weeks or months. Prominences are formed of somewhat cooler solar material. Often the material is ejected into space once the prominence breaks apart.

The Sun is expected to remain in its current Main Sequence stage for another 5 billion years, fusing the remaining hydrogen atoms into helium (the total Main Sequence phase for a star the size of the Sun is 10 billion years). Once the remaining hydrogen has been fused the Sun will develop into a Red Giant. At this point the core of the Sun will be helium. It will be dense enough and hot enough that the contraction will resume (without the hydrogen fusion to push against it) and the helium will fuse into denser elements such as carbon. As the core continues to contract, the outer layers of the Sun will expand and cool – which is why this phase is given the name Red Giant. The outer layers will expand to 40% of the Sun's current size and cool to a shade of red rather than yellow. By the time the Sun is 12.3 billion years old it will have completed the fusion of its helium core, beginning its Planetary Nebulae phase - it's shortest phase.

In the planetary Nebulae phase fusion will have stopped at the Sun's core. All that will remain is the dense, heated, carbon core, and the remaining outer layers which group in a nebulous cloud (i.e., planetary nebulae) around the center. As the outer layers cool they will vent off into space. Much of the Sun's original mass will be gone, but the core will remain. Although cooled and less massive, the core will shine very brightly, which is why this phase has been given the name of White Dwarf.

With time the brightness of the White Dwarf will dim, as the remaining energy from fusion reactions dissipate. The Sun will finish its cycle as a black dwarf – a state in which it has ceased to generate any heat or light.

MERCURY

The closest planet to the Sun – and first of the terrestrial planets) is Mercury. Mercury is the smallest of the planets – only slightly larger than Earth's Moon. It is, however, denser than the Moon. Mercury has a proportionally large core, and is composed of 70% metals (largely iron), and 30% silicate materials. In all, Mercury is only slightly denser than the Earth. Other than being denser than the Earth's Moon, Mercury is fairly similar to it. It is marked by crater holes and ridges extending for hundreds miles across its surface.

Because it is so much closer to the Sun it rotates much more quickly than Earth does. Mercury completes a rotation around the Sun every 88 Earth days, and day on mercury is the equivalent of 59 Earth days.

Mercury has the thinnest atmosphere of any of the planets in the solar system. Its small size results in low gravitational pull. In addition, its close placement to the Sun exposes it to regular solar winds and other disturbances that impact its ability to maintain an atmosphere. The atmosphere that it does have is composed of primarily oxygen (40%), sodium (30%), and hydrogen (20%).

The thin atmosphere on Mercury lends to a volatile climate – there is no force to protect the planet against powerful rays from the Sun, and nothing to hold in the heat after the planet rotates away from the Sun. Normal daytime temperatures on Mercury are around 700 degrees Fahrenheit (400 degrees Celsius), and normal night temperatures are -280 degrees Fahrenheit (-130 degrees Celsius).

VENUS

Venus is the second closest planet to the Sun. In many ways it is similar to Earth- earning it the occasional distinction of being the Earth's "sister planet." Venus is roughly the same size as the Earth, and has a similar density and composition – it has an iron core, surrounding by a rocky semi-solid mantle, and an outer crust composed largely of basalt. In other ways, however, Venus is strikingly different from Earth. It was once believed to be an island paradise (thick clouds obscured its surface from observation), but further studied has revealed harsh conditions on the planet's surface.

One example of this difference is its atmosphere. The atmosphere of Venus is nearly 100 times as thick as Earth's and is composed almost entirely of carbon dioxide – creating quite a hostile environment on the surface. Although astronomers believe Venus to have once been covered in water, heat from the Sun caused it to evaporate long ago. This thick atmosphere results in an exaggerated "greenhouse" effect for the surface of Venus. Heat is absorbed and trapped by the thick atmosphere, with little chance for the surface to cool. As a result, the average surface temperature of Venus is slightly over 850 degrees Fahrenheit (450 degrees Celsius). This makes it the hottest planet in the solar system, despite being only the second closest to the Sun. At temperatures this high, even lead would melt on the planet's surface.

The slow rotation and low atmosphere of Venus also contribute to its harsh environment. Venus rotates at a very slow speed – taking 245 Earth days to circle around its axis one time. Alternatively, Venus is able to orbit around the Sun once in each 225 Earth days. This would make a day on Venus longer than a year there if not for Venus' curios rotation. Venus rotates in the opposite direction of most planets. Because of this fact a day on Venus is only 117 Earth day's long.

This incredibly slow daily rotation doesn't allow for Venus to have a very large magnetic field. This means that unlike Earth – where the magnetic field is useful in protecting the planet's surface against solar flares and ejections – Venus is left open to intense radiation from solar storms. This is likely the reason for its incredibly light atmosphere (solar winds and storms blow away all but the heavy carbon dioxide.

As is the case with Mercury, Venus is not known to have any Moons. It is, however, home to thousands of volcanoes – many of which are still active.

EARTH

Our Earth is the third planet from the Sun, and there are a number of unique aspects of its composition and structure that have allowed for the existence of such abundant life that has not emerged on any of the other known planets. For example, Earth orbits in what is nicknamed the "goldilocks zone." This is the range in which a planet is far enough away from the Sun that water won't evaporate, but close enough that it won't freeze. This perfect positioning allows the abundant liquid water which forms the oceans covering 75% of the planet. It also allows the Earth to maintain a comfortable average temperature of approximately 61 degrees Fahrenheit (16 degrees Celsius). Of course, temperatures can vary from that base on position on the Earth and on seasonal changes.

The Earth is slightly less than 93 million miles (150 million kilometers) away from the Sun. This distance is used in astronomy to measure the distances of objects in space. It is called an Astronomical Unit (AU).

The Earth has a two-part core: the most inner part is a solid nickel-iron mass and is surrounded by a liquid nickel-iron alloy. The inner core is similar in temperature to the surface of the Sun, but the immense pressures pushing from outside the core keep it from melting. Movements within the liquid core region are what cause the Earth's magnetic field. This field provides important protection for the planet, deflecting strong solar winds that would otherwise cause excessive amounts of radiation to the Earth's surface.

The core is surrounded by a molten mantle layer composed largely of silicates, magnesium, and iron. The mantle moves under the power of convection – heating in areas that are closer to the core and then rising closer to the surface of the planet as cooler areas sink back downwards, making room for the cycle to continue. The convection cycle within the mantle pushes on the Earth's crust and results in the movement of tectonic plates and the formation of volcanoes. The main components of the Earth's crust are oxygen, iron, silicon, and magnesium.

The Earth's atmosphere is mainly composed of nitrogen which accounts for about 80% of the atmosphere. The other twenty percent is oxygen. This amount of free oxygen is unique to the Earth, and is not found on any other planet in the solar system. The bulk of atmosphere extends within 100 miles (160 kilometers) above Earth's surface, getting thinner further away from the Earth. Some remnants of atmosphere can be found as far as 370 miles (600 kilometers) above the Earth.

MARS

Mars is the fourth planet from the Sun, and last of the four terrestrial planets. It is oven given the nickname of the "Red Planet" because it appears slightly reddish in color. This is caused by iron and other mineral particles within the soil that have oxidized over time, giving the planet's soil and atmosphere the reddish appearance.

Mars is much smaller than Earth with a diameter only half its size and a volume only one sixth of its size. This gives it a gravitational pull that is only about one third that of the Earth. It orbits at approximately the same speed as the Earth and has a similar axial tilt – resulting in seasonal changes similar to those on Earth.

Despite its smaller size, Mars is home to the largest known mountain in the solar system – Olympus Mons. It is a massive volcano that is believed to still be active. It is over 350 miles (600 kilometers) across and 16 miles (27 kilometers) tall. This far surpasses any geologic features on the Earth which has its highest mountain ranges reaching only 5 miles (9 kilometers) above sea level.

The internal composition of Mars is somewhat similar to Earth – it contains a solid core of iron, nickel, and other dense elements. Despite the presence of several volcanos on its surface (including the Olympus Mons), the mantle of Mars has become relatively cool and is likely the consistency of a soft paste. The crust is composed largely of volcanic basalt covered in a fine, powdery dust. Unlike Earth there are no tectonic plates on Mars – the crust is all one continuous piece that is 30 miles (50 kilometers) thick.

A greater distance from the Sun results in a much cooler temperature on the surface of Mars than the three other terrestrial planets. The average temperature is -80 degrees Fahrenheit (-60 degrees Celsius), and they are known to hit as low as -200 degrees Fahrenheit (-125 degrees Celsius) during the coldest times of the year. This cool temperature makes it nearly impossible for liquid water to exist on the surface of Mars (although it is believed that it once did), although ice exists within the soil and at the poles.

Mars, like Venus, has a very thin atmosphere composed primarily of carbon dioxide (more than 95%). This makes it an unlikely candidate to support life. However, unlike Venus, a day on Mars is similar to a day on Earth – lasting only slightly longer than 24 hours. Its year is much longer though, with the smaller, more distant planet taking 687 Earth days to complete one full revolution around the Sun.

There are two known Moons that orbit the planet Mars called Phobos and Deimos. They are most likely asteroids that were captured by its gravitational field and are some of the smallest natural satellites in the solar system.

ASTEROID BELT

The asteroid belt comprises the region that lies between the orbits of Mars and Jupiter, making it approximately 1 astronomical unit wide. It is more specifically referred to as the main belt to differentiate it from other asteroid clusters within the solar system.

The main belt was discovered in the 18th century when a group of astronomers joined together to search for a rumored "fifth terrestrial planet" that was mathematically predicted should exist within the region. Instead the large asteroid Ceres was discovered by another astronomer outside the group. Initially it was believed to be another planet, but as more and more similar objects were discovered over the course of the century, it soon became apparent that these objects were too small and too numerous to be considered planets. They were given the name asteroids, but are sometimes referred to as minor planets or planetoids.

The asteroid belt includes billions of asteroids that range in size from a few feet to several hundred miles in diameter. Some are large chunks of rock, and others more closely resemble piles of rocky debris loosely held together by their own gravity. While the majority of asteroids are composed of a rocky material, there are also several that are believed to contain more rare metals such as iron, nickel, and titanium.

Despite the staggering number of asteroids contained within the region, if all of the material were gathered into one body it would be only about one quarter of the mass of Earth's Moon. The largest body in the asteroid belt is Ceres. With a diameter of 600 miles (950 kilometers), Ceres is twice as long as the next largest known asteroid (Pallas). This has led Ceres to be given the classification of Dwarf planet, rather than asteroid. Ceres alone accounts for about a third of the mass contained within the asteroid belt.

Astronomers believe that the asteroid belt was developed concurrently with the planets. As gravitational forces and began to form all the dust and rock orbiting the Sun into planets, the gravitational pull from Jupiter disrupted the process for the nearby asteroid belt. Rather than coalescing into a planet, the rocky materials repeatedly collided violently. Other materials were swept away to other parts of the solar system. Rather than a planet forming, millions of unattached asteroids remain. Occasionally, asteroids may break free from the asteroid belt, or be pulled into orbit by other bodies. For the most part, though, they remain in a loose pattern throughout the asteroid belt.

Even though there are so many asteroids they remain very distant from one another. The average distance between any two asteroids is around 600,000 miles (nearly 100,000 kilometers). To put that in perspective, it is approximately twice the distance between the Earth and the Moon – and remember, the asteroids are much smaller than the Moon. In fact, in many cases it would be difficult, when located at one asteroid, to identify the nearest asteroid to that point, as some of them can be only a few feet wide. Because of this distant spacing, ships and satellites are able to easily pass through the asteroid belt without colliding into any asteroids.

JUPITER

Jupiter is the first planet outside the asteroid belt. It is the fifth planet from the Sun, and the first of the gas giants. The term "gas giant" fits Jupiter particularly well because it is more than twice as massive as all of the other planets in the solar system combined. It is similar in composition to the Sun – only much smaller. Had Jupiter been around 80 times more massive, it would have developed into a star of its own. Because of this some consider it to be just as much a failed star as it is a large planet. It holds the distinction of being the fourth brightest objects in the solar system (following behind the Sun, Moon, and Venus).

Despite its incredible size, Jupiter rotates faster than any other planet in the solar system. It takes approximately 10 hours for Jupiter to complete a full rotation as compared to Earth's 24 hours. The speed at which it rotates causes the planet to bulge out around the equator, giving it a slightly oblong shape. The circumference of Jupiter is 7% larger when taken around the equator than it is when taken from the planet's north to south poles. In contrast, Jupiter has a year much longer than that of Earth's, taking nearly 12 of Earth's years to complete a single orbit about the Sun.

With an average distance of 480 million miles (800 million kilometers) from the Sun, Jupiter receives very little heat from it. Rather, heat from convection and pressure within the planet keeps it from freezing over. As a result, even though Jupiter is a gas giant composed of mostly layered gaseous, plasma, and liquid elements, its "surface" (as defined by scientists - only the core of the planet is actually solid) is much colder than Earth. The average surface temperature on Jupiter is -230 degrees Fahrenheit (-145 degrees Celsius).

Not much is known about the core of the planet, although it is believed to be rocky. The remainder of the planet is composed of primarily hydrogen (accounting for about 90% of its mass) and helium (accounting for about 10% of its mass). The core is surrounded by a fluid, metallic hydrogen layer, and a molecular hydrogen atmosphere. The fluid hydrogen layer is unique in its metallic behavior. On Earth hydrogen is a poor conductive material and cannot behave as a metal. However, within the planet Jupiter it does. It is theorized that this is possible due to tremendous pressures within the planet that allow electrons to break free from atoms and move freely throughout the fluid region of the planet.

The metallic behavior of the hydrogen, combined with the rapid rotational speed of the planet, causes Jupiter to have a tremendously powerful magnetic field – nearly 20,000 times stronger than that of Earth's. The field extends millions of miles out from the planet, and regularly blasts waves of radiation towards Jupiter's Moons in quantities more than 1,000 times the lethal dose for a human. The effects of this powerful magnetic field are also seen in unique surface conditions on Jupiter.

Beyond its fluid hydrogen layer, Jupiter contains a liquid hydrogen layer, followed by an atmosphere of primarily hydrogen. Jupiter is known for the bands of color that characterize its surface, and the Great Red Spot – a storm that has lasted hundreds of years without stopping. The bands of color are caused by powerful atmospheric winds that circle around the planet. The white bands are clouds of frozen ammonia. Darker clouds represent other elements found in trace amounts in the atmosphere such as sulfur, methane and water vapor.

The Great Red Spot is a violent hurricane so massive that it is visible through telescopes from Earth. It rotates counter-clockwise and is so large that it takes nearly six days to rotate completely. The most likely reason that the storm has persisted for as long as it has (nearly 300 years) is that unlike hurricanes on Earth, the storm never passes over land, only the liquid and gaseous hydrogen that compose the planet.

Its tremendous size and gravitational pull have afforded Jupiter at least 63 Moons, the most well-known of which are Ganymede, Io, Callisto and Europa. They are known as the Galilean satellites because they were discovered by Galileo himself, and used as evidence that the Earth was not the center of the universe.

Ganymede is distinguished as being the largest Moon in the solar system. It is even larger than the planet Mercury, and is the only Moon large enough to have its own magnetic field. The Moon Io is unique because it is the most volcanically active body in the solar system and one of the few Moons to have volcanic activity at all. Europa is composed largely of water and ice, potentially containing twice amount of water as Earth's oceans do.

In addition to its 63 Moons, Jupiter also has three very faint rings that lie about its equator. They are called the main ring, the halo, and the gossamer ring, and are composed of small, dust particles.

SATURN

Saturn is the second of the solar system's gas giants, and as the sixth planet from the Sun it is the furthest planet that can be observed with the naked eye. As a gas giant, Saturn shares a number of characteristics with the planet Jupiter (and with the Sun), but it has many features that are its own also.

Saturn is the least dense planet in the solar system. It has a density of less than .7 grams/cubic centimeter – that's half of what the density of Jupiter is. With such a low density, Saturn would literally float in water if a large enough body of it existed. It is able to maintain such a low density because the planet is primarily composed of gaseous elements, having no solid outer crust like the four terrestrial planets do.

Similarly to Jupiter, Saturn has a very rapid rotation speed. It has the second shortest day of all the planets in the solar system, estimated at approximately 10 hours and 34 minutes (compared to Jupiter's 9 hours and 56 minutes). This speed had to be measured by observing the planet's strong magnetic field (more than 578 times the strength of that of the Earth) because there is no way to observe ground conditions and determine the exact speed. A year on Saturn is 29.5 Earth years.

As is the case with Jupiter, this fast rotation speed combined with the planet's incredibly low density causes the planet to bulge around its equator. This bulging has the result that Saturn is a full ten percent smaller on its polar diameter (from the North to the south poles) than it is around its equatorial diameter (from one point on the equator to another directly across from it), and this causes the planet appear to have the shape of a slightly flattened ball.

Internally Saturn is very similar to Jupiter – largely composed of hydrogen and helium in a primarily gaseous and liquid state. The rocky core would have been the first part of the planet to form – it's believed to be at least 10 times the size of Earth. With this much dense, rocky mass the hydrogen and helium atoms were then attracted to the planet to create the outer layers that are visible today.

Surrounding this rocky core is a layer of liquid metallic hydrogen which fades into liquid molecular hydrogen. Eventually the layer of molecular hydrogen fades into a gaseous hydrogen atmosphere. Unlike terrestrial planets, the layers of Saturn's internal structure are not clearly defined, instead changing gradually from one form to another at no specific location. The hydrogen has a rich amount of helium mingled throughout. The overall composition is approximately 75% hydrogen to 25% helium. The upper atmosphere contains traces of other elements such as ammonium and methane, as does Jupiter.

Saturn is considered to be one of the windiest planets. Although the surface winds do not manifest in obvious colored bands as they do on Jupiter, massive storms will often break out on its surface with speeds clocked at up to (1800 kilometers per second). For comparison, consider that the maximum wind speeds that have been observed on the Earth are a mere 400 kilometers per second.

Great amounts of heat and pressure exist within the core of Saturn, yet there is also a fair amount of ice present in its outer layers. The average temperature is -280 degrees Fahrenheit (-175 degrees Celsius), although the core can reach temperatures above 21,000 degrees Fahrenheit (11,700 degrees Celsius).

There are 62 identified Moons that orbit about Saturn. The vast arrays of Moons display unique features in their compositions, orbits, and sizes. The first of Saturn's Moons to be discovered, and the most well-known of them, was Titan. Titan is the second largest Moon in the Solar System (second to Jupiter's Moon Ganymede). It has a nitrogen-rich atmosphere similar to Earths, but at ten times its size. Titan is large enough that it influences the orbits of other Moons that draw near to it.

Most of Saturn's Moons are frozen. Many smaller Moons orbit in directions opposite of the larger Moons. Some Moons orbit inside of Saturn's famed rings, and others simply pass through them during the course of their orbits. At least 16 of Saturn's Moons have been discovered to be tidally locked to the planet, as Earth's Moon is. Still some planets have chaotic orbits and rotations as results of recent collisions.

The most distinctive feature of the planet Saturn is its massive, icy rings. Galileo was the first to discover these rings, although with the limited view of his telescope they appeared to him to be two Moons orbiting on either side of the planet. In fact, there are two Moons that orbit with the rings, serving to keep a division between different layers of rings, but the rings themselves are an incredibly spectacle spanning over 75,000 miles (120,000 kilometers) outward from the planet. Despite the long range of the rings, they maintain an average thickness of only 12 miles (20 kilometers).

The particles composing the rings vary in size from small dust particles to a few the size of small Moons. They are believed to be the remnants of comets, asteroids, and Moons that collided and shattered. Each ring has a different orbital speed.

URANUS

Uranus follows Saturn in distance from the Sun. It is the first of the "ice giants." Much like the gas giants, Uranus has a high concentration of hydrogen and helium in its composition. However, the cold temperatures that characterize the planet give it a formation more of ice than gases and liquids like Jupiter and Saturn. Uranus is far enough away from the Earth that it is not visible to the naked eye. It was first discovered by Sir William Herschel in 1781, making it the first planet to be discovered by telescope.

The most striking feature of Uranus is its unique axial tilt. Uranus has an axial tilt of 98 degrees, which gives it the appearance of rolling perpendicular to all of the other planets. The most likely explanation for this dramatic tilt is a collision with an Earth-sized body at some point since its formation.

Because of this dramatic axial tilt, seasonal changes on Uranus are very dramatic. For a quarter of the year Uranus will be angled so that its entire northern pole faces the Sun, while the southern pole is left in complete darkness. Then for another quarter of the year the opposite will happen, with the southern pole completely facing towards the Sun while the northern pole is left in complete darkness. The severity of these seasons is enhanced by the fact that a year on Uranus is much longer than one on Earth. It takes Uranus slightly more than 84 Earth years to complete one revolution around the Sun. A year of this length means that each of its seasons last a total of 21 years.

In addition to rotating on its side, Uranus also has a retrograde rotation- meaning that it rotates in the opposite direction as Earth and a majority of the other seven planets. A day on Uranus lasts for 17 hours and 14 minutes of Earth time.

The internal structure of Uranus is similar to that of Jupiter and Saturn in that it is not formed of rigid layers. Instead each layer gradually forms into the next. The core of the planet is composed of heavy metals, and is about the size of the Earth. From there the primary elements are methane, water, and ammonia in an icy mantle layer. The high concentration of methane in the mantle is what gives Uranus its characteristic blue color. Beyond this icy mantle is the lower layer of the atmosphere – primarily composed of hydrogen and helium.

Uranus has a maximum surface temperature of -240 degrees Fahrenheit (-150 degrees Celsius). Although it doesn't maintain the coldest temperatures of any planet, it does hit the coldest temperature of any planet, with a minimum temperature of around -370 degrees Fahrenheit (-210 degrees Celsius). In addition to these frigid temperatures, Uranus's extreme seasonal changes and unique magnetic field (which has its own axial tilt of about 60 degrees) contribute to strong winds and storms on the planet's surface.

Like its neighboring planets, Uranus has a series of narrow rings around its equator that vary in color (some appear red, others blue or other darker colors). At least thirteen rings have been discovered, but more may still be found as investigations of the planet continue.

Uranus has 27 known Moons. The first discovered of these, and the largest, are called Oberon and Titania. All of Uranus's Moons have a partial rock, partial ice composition. Many of them are most likely asteroids that were captured into its gravitational field. In some places the small Moons are so close to each other that astronomers are surprised that they haven't already collided with one another.

NEPTUNE

With the reclassification of Pluto as a dwarf planet, Neptune is the final planet in the solar system. It is the eighth planet from the Sun and is an ice giant like Uranus. As the furthest planet in the solar system, Neptune is 30 times further away from the Sun than the Earth is. It has the longest year of any planet – 165 Earth years. This slow movement caused it to be mistakenly identified as simply another star when observed by Galileo. It was not discovered as a planet until 1846. It took until 2011 for it to complete its first full rotation from the time of its discovery.

Neptune has a similar composition to Uranus. It has a rocky core about the size of the Earth. The core is surrounded by a slushy mantle of methane ice, water, and ammonia. Its atmosphere is primarily hydrogen helium and methane, giving it a bluish tint. Neptune also has five rings – each named for an astronomer that made important discoveries about the planet Neptune. The rings are primarily composed of dust, and are most likely the remains of a destroyed Moon.

There are 13 confirmed Moons of Neptune. The largest and most well-known of these Moons is Triton. Triton is the only one of Neptune's Moon's that has a spherical shape – all of the others are irregular. It is thought to have originally been a dwarf planet that was captured by Neptune's gravitational field.

As a Moon, Triton has many unique features. Although it is known to be one of the coldest places in the solar system – even colder than the planet it orbits – water was seen spewing from its surface, making it likely that an ocean lies beneath the icy outer layers. Also unique to Triton is that it is the largest Moon in the solar system with a retrograde movement – meaning it rotates opposite to the planet it orbits. Because of Triton's unique orbit, it will one day move close enough to Neptune to be torn apart by its gravity. Seasons have even been discovered on Triton.

Very little heat or light from the Sun reaches Neptune. As a result it has the coldest average temperature on any planet. The average temperature at the top of its atmosphere is -350 degrees Fahrenheit (-210 degrees Celsius). The planet has an axial tilt similar to Earth's. As a result there is a temperature variation of around 50 degrees Fahrenheit on the planet between summer and winter seasons (which would each last around 41 years).

PLUTO AND OTHER DWARF PLANETS

At the time of its discovery in 1930 Pluto was considered to be the 9th planet in the Solar System. However, the discovery of additional similar bodies orbiting the Sun nearby caused it to be downgraded to a dwarf planet. Dwarf planets are bodies that are caught orbiting the Sun, as the true planets are. They are large enough to have taken on a roughly spherical shape – which distinguishes them from asteroids that can be found in any shape or size throughout the solar system.

Another difference between regular planets and dwarf planets is that dwarf planets do not have sufficient size and gravitational field to clear themselves a path of orbit. This means that other objects are free to pass through and around their orbits undisturbed- potentially causing collisions. This is not the case with true planets whose gravitational fields pull objects in their path into orbit or cause them to break apart. For example, this is why Ceres (the largest object in the asteroid belt) is considered to be a dwarf planet. It is too large to be considered simply an asteroid. However it is closely surrounded by other asteroids and has no clear orbital path of its own. Nor does it have sufficient gravitational pull to create one.

The rest of the dwarf planets that have been discovered lay beyond the planet Neptune in a region that has come to be known as the Kuiper Belt. The Kuiper belt is a disk shaped area beyond the orbit of Neptune where icy bodies and comets orbit. It is thought that there may be billions of icy dwarf planets similar to Pluto that are waiting to be discovered. Currently, however, Pluto is the one that we know the most about.

Due to its great distance from the Sun, Pluto is very cold. Its average temperature falls near -400 degrees Fahrenheit (-240 degrees Celsius). The temperature on Pluto does vary at different points in its orbit, however, because Pluto has a much more eccentric (less circular) orbit than any of the major planets. In fact, Pluto's orbit is so extreme that it intersects with the orbit of Neptune, and Pluto was actually closer to the Sun than Neptune was for a period of about 20 years in the 1900's.

Pluto is very small. It has a diameter less than one fifth the size of the Earth's, making it about the width of half of the United States. The gravitational pull is only about one fifteenth the strength of the Earth's. This characteristic is true of other dwarf planets, none of which are bigger than the size of the Earth's Moon.

In terms of composition, Pluto bears more resemblance to the terrestrial planets of the inner solar system that it does to the nearby gas and ice giants. The primary elements in its composition are nitrogen, methane, and water, almost all in frozen icy forms. Based on the calculated density of Pluto, astronomers believe it to contain a dense core composed of rocky material that is surrounded by these ices.

The atmosphere on Pluto varies depending on the relative location of its orbit. During the time when Pluto draws closest to the Sun it warms enough to generate a primarily nitrogen based atmosphere similar to that of the Earths. However, once it draws further away from the Sun again, the cold temperatures cause the atmosphere to freeze and contract so that it has little or no atmosphere until the temperatures warm again.

Pluto has a longer year than any of the major planets, taking nearly 250 years to complete a single orbit around the Sun. This means that astronomer's will not have observed a full year for the planet Pluto until the year 2178.

The majority of dwarf planets have Moons, and Pluto is no exception. There are four Moons that orbit Pluto, the most famous of which is Charon. Some believe that Pluto and Charon should be considered a "planet system" of their own because of how linked their orbits are. Charon is around half the size that Pluto is, and the two are tidally locked to each other. Charon lies incredibly close to Pluto (just over 12,000 miles), and does not truly orbit around it. Rather, the two both orbit around a point that lies between them.

SUMMARY

Planet	Position from Sun	Type	Average Temp	Internal Composition	Atmospheric Composition	Length of Year	Planet	Moons
Mercury	1	Terrestrial	700 F 400 C	Iron and silicates	Oxygen, Sodium, and Hydrogen	88 Days	59 Days	None
Venus	2	Terrestrial	850 F 450 C	Iron and silicates	Carbon Dioxide	245 Days	117 Days	None
Earth	3	Terrestrial	61 F 16 C	Nickle, Iron, Oxygen	Nitrogen, Oxygen	365 Days	24 Hours	1
Mars	4	Terrestrial	-80 F -60 C	Iron, Basalt	Carbon Dioxide	Just over 24 Hours	687 Days	2 - Phobos and Diemos
Jupiter	5	Gas Giant	-230 F -145 C	Rocky core surrounded by Hydrogen and Helium	Hydrogen, Helium	12 Years	10 Hours	63 including Ganymede, Callisto, Io, and Europa
Saturn	6	Gas Giant	-280 F -175 C	Rocky core surrounded by Hydrogen and Helium	Hydrogen, Helium	29.5 Years	10.5 Hours	62 including its most famous – Titan

Uranus	7	Ice Giant	-240 F -150 C	Methane, Water, Ammonia	Hydrogen, Helium	84 Years	17 Hours	27 – the largest are Oberon and Titania
Neptune	8	Ice Giant	-350 F -210 C	Rocky core surrounded by Methane, Ice, and Ammonia	Hydrogen, Helium, Methane	165 Years	16 Hours	13 – the most famous is Triton
Pluto	9	Dwarf Planet	-400 F -240 C	Nitrogen, Methane, Water	Very thin Methane	248 Years	6.4 Days	4 – the most famous is Charon

PLANETS OUTSIDE OF OUR SOLAR SYSTEM

EXOPLANETS

Just as the Sun has planets orbiting around it – creating this solar system – other stars throughout the galaxy have been discovered to have bodies orbiting around them as well. These have come to be known as exoplanets or extrasolar planets. Exoplanets are essentially any planet that orbits a star other than the Sun. Although these were theorized to exist for many centuries, none were verified to exist until 1992. Since that time, however, the number of known exoplanets has grown to nearly 2000.

Early discoveries of exoplanets were primarily gas giants larger even than Jupiter, simply because they are the easiest to detect. Further discoveries have proven that there are many terrestrial planets in existence throughout the universe as well. It is now believed that the majority of stars have at least one planet in orbit around them. Many hundreds have been confirmed as solar systems in their own right, with five or more planets of varying compositions in orbit around them.

The ultimate goal of exoplanet research is to discover other Earth-like planets. Although no planets have yet been discovered that support life as abundantly as Earth does, with time more and more have been discovered with similar features such as terrestrial composition, ability to sustain liquid water, or livable temperatures.

DETECTION OF EXOPLANETS

Due to the difficulty in detecting exoplanets, the vast majority of them have been discovered within the Milky Way Galaxy. Both direct and indirect methods can be used to confirm the existence of an exoplanet, although indirect methods are typically more successful. Direct detection is done through infrared imaging to directly view the existence of another body orbiting a star. Planets discovered through this method are generally very distant from their central star, and are very large gas giants.

The combination of these two characteristics allows the planet to be distinguished from the star in images, but only accounts for a portion of exoplanets. Typically an exoplanet shines less than one millionth of the brightness of its star, making them very difficult to detect from Earth. Less than 5% of exoplanets can be detected through direct imaging, which is why several indirect methods of detection have been developed as well.

One form of indirect detection is an examination of Doppler shifts called Doppler spectroscopy. A planet orbiting a star will cause minute changes in the position of that star, and those changes can be observed from Earth. This method analyzes minute changes in a stars radial velocity to determine the size of an object that is orbiting around it. Doppler spectroscopy is used in detecting a majority of exoplanets. Its main downfall is that it cannot determine the exact size of the exoplanet. It can only determine the minimum mass of the exoplanet that would cause the change in radial velocity.

Another common form of indirect detection is the transit method. When an exoplanet's orbit crosses between the star and Earth then the star will appear to grow dimmer from the perspective of Earth (the planet will be blocking a small amount of light from reaching the Earth). By measuring regular increases and decreases in the brightness of a star over time, the existence of an exoplanet can be inferred. This method is considered to be less reliable than Doppler spectroscopy, and often needs to be considered along with other evidence before it is considered conclusive.

 Our Galaxy and Other Galaxies: Contents and Structure

OUR GALAXY: THE MILKY WAY

Our solar system is only a small part of a larger grouping of stars called a galaxy. A galaxy is a system of billions of stars that are held together by gravitational forces. In many cases the source of this gravitational force is a large black hole at the center of the system. The galaxy in which our solar system resides is called the Milky Way Galaxy.

Viewed from space the Milky Way would appear as a giant spiral of stars and dust moving through the universe. The solar system in which our Sun resides is on the outskirts of one of the spirals known as the Orion Arm. The exact size of the galaxy is continually changing because new stars are constantly being formed, while old stars are regularly passing away. Additionally, stars from nearby galaxies are also consumed by the galaxy's gravitational pull and molded in as a part of it.

Currently, the Milky Way is composed of approximately 200 billion stars, most of which are not visible to the naked eye from Earth. Many of these stars are similar to the

Sun, but differences in size and composition allow for several different types of stars to evolve throughout the galaxy.

TYPES OF STARS

All stars are composed primarily of hydrogen and helium, like the Sun. At different stages in their existence stars will have varying ratios of these two elements, and shine at varying levels of brightness. Towards the end of a stars life cycle fusion may result in the presence of other heavier elements, but for the vast majority of the time, stars exist by burning hydrogen through fusion. A star's mass will determine the length of its lifecycle, and the nature of its final stages as a star.

Protostar: Before a star has gained sufficient mass and gravitational force to start nuclear fusion at its core it is known as a protostar. This is the beginning stage a star formation, and occurs as large clouds of molecular dust and elements begin to collapse inwards under gravitational pressures.

Main Sequence Stars: A star spends the majority of its life as a main sequence star. This is the current stage of the Sun. Stars in main sequence are characterized by energy release through hydrogen fusion. The size of main sequence stars vary from 8% of the size of the Sun, up to around 100 times the size of the Sun. A star can remain in this state of hydrogen fusion for several billion years before its fuel source becomes exhausted.

Red Giant: Main Sequence Stars are kept in balance by opposing forces of gravity and fusion. While fusion releases energy and pushes outward on the matter, gravity pulls back inwards. Once the hydrogen fuel has been consumed, fusion stops and the balance between these forces is upset. Stars in this stage of evolution are known as Red Giant stars. The ending of hydrogen fusion allows gravitational pressures to pull the star inwards. This results in increasing pressures and temperatures at its core which generate helium fusion. As fusion renews, pressures again push outward causing the star to expand several times its original size. It is known as the Red Giant phase because in this stage, the star will begin to emit a reddish glow rather than the yellow which characterizes the main sequence.

White Dwarf: After a star reaches the red giant phase, the remainder of its life is largely determined by mass. For stars with a mass similar to the Sun's the final stage is as a white dwarf. This occurs once helium fusion ceases at the core of the star. At this point the star will have expanded in the red giant phase, and the excess matter that is not a part of the core will be released into space. This leaves behind a very hot ball composed largely of carbon. Remaining heat from the fusion process causes the white dwarf star to shine brightly, even though there are no further reactions occurring. It takes millions of years for a white dwarf to cool to levels where they cease to shine.

Black Dwarf: A black dwarf is the theoretical term for white dwarfs that have cooled to levels where they no longer emit light. This term is still only theoretical, however, because scientists calculate that it would take tens of billions of years for a white dwarf to evolve into a black dwarf. Even stars created at the very beginning of the universe would not yet have been able to reach this stage.

Red Dwarf: The majority of stars in the galaxy are red dwarf stars. This type of star is far smaller than the Sun – they range from around 8%-50% the size of the Sun. As other stars do, red dwarfs begin as protostars, or large clouds of molecular dust that begin to collapse inwards and rotate. The difference is that because of their much smaller mass, red dwarfs create hydrogen fusion at a much slower rate than a normal main sequence star. Because of this they are much less bright. However, they also have a much longer life span than main sequence stars. Whereas main sequence stars consume their hydrogen cores within 10 billion years, red dwarfs will continue the fusion process for trillions of years. Once their supply of hydrogen is exhausted, red dwarfs will become blue dwarfs.

Blue Dwarf: Blue dwarf is the theoretical term for red dwarf stars that have exhausted their hydrogen fuel. Because red dwarfs continue in a state of hydrogen fusion for trillions of years, none have yet reached this stage- which is why it is still a theoretical classification. The theory behind blue dwarf stars is that once hydrogen fusion stops in a red dwarf star, rather than progressing to a red giant stage like main sequence stars, the star will maintain its size and increase in temperature instead. This increase in temperature results in the star appearing to glow in a bluer tone.

Brown Dwarf: Some stars don't even have sufficient mass to reach the red dwarf stage. These stars are known as brown dwarfs. Brown dwarf stars are sometimes considered to be failed stars because in many aspects they resemble a large planet more than a star. While main sequence stars are formed as interstellar dust collapses inwards and generates pressure, the pressure levels in a brown dwarf star are never high enough to ignite hydrogen fusion at the core. Despite the lack of fusion, however, brown dwarfs are considered stars because they still generate their own light in the red and infrared spectrums (unlike planets). Brown dwarfs range from around 13-20 times the size of Jupiter.

Neutron Star: There are also many stars that are even more massive than the Sun. Stars that have a mass that is around 130-200% the size of the Sun will not reach a white dwarf stage. Instead they undergo a massive explosion known as a supernova. The remnants of these explosions are called neutron stars. Essentially, the remaining core after the supernova will be so pressurized and densely packed that all of the protons and electrons that compose the core will fuse together. This leaves behind a unique star composed entirely of neutrons. The amount of gravity generated by these stars is billions of times the strength of that experienced on Earth.

Blue Giant Stars or Supergiant Stars: Stars that are several dozens of times the size of our Sun are known as blue giants or supergiant stars. These are the largest, brightest stars in the universe. They burn at temperatures exceeding 20,000-50,000 Kelvin (which is around 30-100 times the heat of the Sun). These extreme temperatures give them a bluer tone than other stars. Blue giants give off tens of thousands of times the amount of energy that the Sun does, but they have much shorter life spans. When these types of stars reach the end of their lives they will detonate in a massive supernova, often leaving behind a black hole.

Supernova: There are two basic types of supernovae: Type I Supernovae and Type II Supernovae. A Type I supernova occurs in white dwarfs that are no more than 1.4 solar masses, and that are locked in a binary system (in other words, a white dwarf and another star orbiting one other at a common center). Because of the white dwarfs strong gravitational pull it will be able to pull mass from the other star. This is called accretion, and will increase the pressure and mass of the white dwarf.

Remember that white dwarfs develop because all hydrogen and helium at the core has fused to carbon, but there isn't sufficient pressure to fuse any further. Once the white dwarf reaches a size greater than 1.4 solar masses the carbon will again ignite and cause a supernova explosion. The amount of energy released in a supernova is bright enough to obscure the rest of the galaxy for several minutes, and totals to more energy and radiation than the Sun will give off in its entire lifetime.

A Type II supernova occurs in larger stars than a Type I supernova, with sizes ranging from around 8-15 solar masses. Neutron stars and black holes are the results of Type II supernova. They are caused when the star exhausts its hydrogen and helium fuel, and heavier elements begin building up at the core. The amount of pressure and heat at the core at this point causes it to begin to collapse under its own gravitational force and energy and light explode outwards in a supernova.

HOW STARS ARE CLASSIFIED

Clusters

One way in which stars can be classified is by the manner in which they group together, or "cluster." The primary forms of clusters are open clusters and globular clusters. Clusters are groupings of stars that are held together by their own mutual gravitational pulls. They orbit about the centers of galaxies and tend to be the same ages – having formed from the same clouds of interstellar dust.

The older form of clusters is globular clusters. These clusters are also larger, typically containing thousands to hundreds of thousands of stars within them. They form in symmetrical ways, and at this point contain primarily aging stars such as red giants. Globular clusters no longer form in the Milky Way galaxy due to its age.

In contrast to globular clusters, open clusters are smaller groupings of stars – typically in the hundreds. These stars are younger and brighter than the stars of globular clusters. Open clusters are found in the spiral arms of many galaxies, and are still forming within the spirals of the Milky Way Galaxy.

Populations

During World War II much of the world's attention was turned away from astronomical research. However, astronomer Walter Baade was a German-born scientist living in California and was restricted from aiding in the war research. This left him with much open time to pursue his own studies, and he focused his work on discussing two broad categories of stars which are now called Population I and Population II stars. Later in the 1970's a third category – Population III stars- was added to his model.

Population I stars are primarily younger and more metal rich stars. These stars are found in the main disc of the galaxy. In astronomical terms, a metal is classified as any element other than hydrogen and helium. These are the two elements that compose the majority of the galaxy, and even they have been discovered to behave in metallic ways under extreme pressures within stars. This makes it simple to refer to everything heavier as a metal.

Population I stars tend to have more uniform and circular orbits that keep them on the main plane of the galaxy. The stars are loosely bound together in open clusters. They range in metal abundance from .1 to 2.5 times the concentration of our Sun.

In contrast, Population II stars have less than one hundredth the metal concentration as the Sun. These are the older, dimmer stars of the galaxy. Many of the stars that fall into this classification are more than 10 billion years old. Population II stars tend to cluster in an irregular sphere around the center of the galaxy, or floating in a halo around the outer edges of it.

The older age of population II stars is likely the cause of their low metal content. Population I stars are potentially remnants of supernovae or other astronomical phenomenon following the creation of heavier metals. Population II stars were born in a time when heavier metals were scarcely found throughout the galaxy, leaving them without an abundance of these materials at the time of their formation.

Population III stars are still mostly theoretical. These are stars that are even more metal poor than are population II stars, with their amount of metal composition being less than one millionth the amount of the Suns. Stars such as these would be composed of purely un-recycled material, making them the oldest in the galaxy – having originated close to the time of its formation. It's possible that stars such as these have not been discovered because they have simply all burned out and become other forms of stars. It is also possible that movements and deposits from other stars have caused population III stars to incorrectly appear to be population II stars with low amount of metals.

Magnitude and Luminosity

A third way that stars are commonly classified is based on their magnitude and luminosity. These values are used in one of the most famous diagrams in astronomy – the Hertzsprung-Russel Diagram or HR Diagram. The HR Diagram is graph which plots the absolute magnitude against the color of a star (its spectral type), or plots its temperature against its luminosity. An HR Diagram that plots temperature against luminosity is called a theoretical HR Diagram. One which plots absolute magnitude against spectral type is called an observational HR Diagram or color-magnitude diagram.

The absolute magnitude of a star is the brightness that it would have if it were ten parsec away from the Earth. It is important to determine the absolute magnitude (brightness) because the relative distances between stars varies so greatly that they cannot be compared to each other. For example, from the perspective of the Earth the Sun will always be the brightest star in the sky, but this is simply because it is the closest. If another star were at an equal distance as the Sun it would shine brighter or dimmer based on its own properties. When all stars are considered in terms of their absolute magnitude instead of their apparent magnitude (the actual brightness they appear at) astronomers can have a clearer picture of their characteristics.

The luminosity of a star is measured as the amount of energy that it emits. Although it is typically measured in Watts, luminosity is generally stated by solar multiples (i.e., a luminosity of 2 would indicate a star that emitted two times the amount of energy as the Sun). Luminosity and absolute magnitude are proportional to each other, so they are often interchangeable as measures.

A star's spectral type refers to its classification on the Harvard Spectral Classification scheme. The scheme was first created at Harvard in the 1800s, although it has been updated since then. This classification takes advantage of the relationship between the temperatures of stars and the color that they appear as. The hottest stars appear whiter or bluer, and the cooler stars appear closer to red or orange. There are seven spectral classifications in this system:

Classification	Color	Temperature (Kelvin)
O	Blue	More than 28,000 K
B	Blue-White	10,000-28,000 K
A	White	7,500-10,000 K
F	Yellow-White	5,000-7,500 K
G	Yellow	5,000-6,000 K

| K | Orange-Red | 3,500-5,000 K |
| M | Red | Less than 3,500 K |

Type O stars are the hottest and brightest stars. There are very few main sequence stars that fall into this classification, but some do exist. Type O stars are the only stars that have a spectral signature that indicates that presence of ionized helium. Among main sequence stars, type O stars are the rarest form.

Type B stars will shine bright and blue. Because of the amount of energy they emit they tend to have relatively short lives compared to other stars. They tend to be located in areas near other type O and B stars. Nearly a third of the stars visible to the naked eye are classified as type B stars, although in absolute terms they are one of the rarer forms of stars.

Type A stars are bright and white shining stars. Their main distinguishing characteristic is their prominent helium absorption lines when viewed using spectroscopy. Because of how brightly they shine type A stars include some of the most famous stars in the sky, such as Vega, the fifth brightest star in the sky and most studied after the Sun.

Type F stars include many main sequence and some giant stars. They shine yellow, with a brightness close to that of the Sun. Their spectral lines are more likely to indicate metals. One example of a popular type F star is Polaris – the North Star.

Type G stars have the distinction of including the Sun. Many main sequence stars fall into the category of type G stars, as well as a number of giant stars. Supergiant stars pass through a phase as type G stars, however it is considered an unstable range for a supergiant star. These stars also typically have a larger than average composition of metal or heavy elements.

Type K stars are typically cooler and dimmer than the Sun, resulting in an orange color. They include one in every eight main sequence stars, and giant K-type stars are also fairly common. Stars such as these are likely to include planets within the habitable zone, making them some of the highest probabilities for supporting life. Because they shine so dimly, they have a long life span than the Sun.

Type M stars are the coolest star types, which allows for more complex molecules to be able to form within them. Nearly three in every four main sequence stars is a type M star, however because they have such a low temperature and luminosity, they are nearly impossible to see with the naked eye. In addition to being such an important component of main sequence stars, the type M classification primarily includes red dwarfs.

The color, magnitude, luminosity, and temperature of a star change at it progresses throughout its lifecycle. The result is that when a star is plotted on the HR Diagram it can be roughly determined what stage that particular star is in based on the combination of those four characteristics. The following is a simplified version of an HR Diagram that shows where four main types of stars would be located: red giants and supergiants in the top right, giants below that, main sequence stars running in a slope from top left to bottom right, and white dwarfs in the bottom left corner.

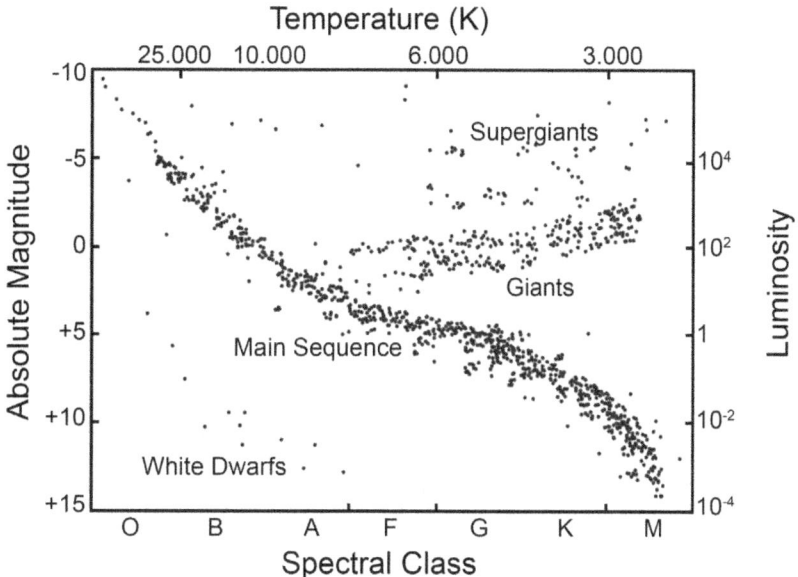

As a point of reference, consider where the Sun would fall on the HR Diagram. Our Sun lies in the line of main sequence stars in the G spectral class due to its yellow color. Because luminosity has a ranking relative to the Sun, the luminosity (the measurement on the right side of the graph) would be 1. The temperature of the Sun is nearly 5,800 Kelvin, and its absolute magnitude is 4.8.

This information places the Sun on the lower-right side of the graph, beneath the giants and supergiants of the galaxy. Interestingly the Sun is thought to have a higher absolute magnitude than nearly 80 percent of the stars in the Milky Way Galaxy. However, most of the stars that have a lower absolute magnitude than the Sun are not visible to the naked eye.

OTHER PHENOMENON IN THE GALAXY

Black Holes

Black Holes are among the most powerful forces in the universe. Essentially, a black hole is a very dense region of space that exerts a powerful gravitational pull. They have such strong gravitational force that not even light is able to escape from it, which is where the name black hole came from. Because of this, black holes cannot technically be seen. Their existence can only be inferred based on the movements of objects that are surrounding the black hole. There are two common types of black holes: stellar black holes and supermassive black holes.

Stellar black holes are the type of black holes that are created when a star detonates in a supernova. As the star ceases hydrogen fusion and begins collapsing due to its gravity, its density will increase dramatically. The amount of gravitational pull exerted by a mass is proportional to its size, so as the same amount of mass is packed into a small and smaller area, the gravitational pull increases to the point where nothing – including light – can escape. Some black holes are known to pack more mass than even the Sun contains into a space the size of an atom. This is how black holes achieve their formidable gravitational fields. There are billions of stellar black holes in the Milky Way galaxy alone.

Supermassive black holes are similar to stellar black holes, but they are much larger. While stellar black holes contain about three times the mass of the Sun, supermassive black holes can be anywhere from hundreds of times the mass of the Sun to millions of times the mass of the Sun. Although their origins are unclear, what is known is that supermassive black holes lie at the centers of galaxies. They are the forces that hold the galaxies together. The supermassive black hole at the center of the Milky Way galaxy is estimated to contain around 4 million times the mass of the Sun.

There are two main parts that make up a black hole: the singularity and the event horizon. The singularity of a black hole is the single point at which all of its mass is centered. All of the mass contained within a black hole is drawn to the singularity, and it continues to be drawn inwards towards it. Ultimately a black hole will move towards having an infinite mass concentrated at this single point.

The event horizon of a black hole is the outer edge at which light can no longer escape from the black hole. Once an object crosses the event horizon it cannot leave. This region is called the event horizon because beyond this point the events that occur within the black hole are unknown. Since no light escapes, any information about the inner workings of the black hole must be inferred or theorized.

A common misconception about black holes is that objects can be "sucked" into them. In fact, objects fall into black holes as a result of their immense gravitational forces (i.e., "sucking" implies a vacuum effect whereas black holes operate based on gravity). In many ways black holes are quite similar to any other cosmic object. If the Sun were to be replaced by a black hole of the same mass, the solar system would continue to function with all of the planets continuing in their same orbits. The unique aspect of black holes is simply their incredible density and gravity. As long as an object stays outside of the event horizon, it can continue to rotate about the black hole as it would any other object.

Quasar

Quasars are some of the furthest objects away from our solar system that can be seen. They are among the brightest objects in the universe, emitting enough energy to overshadow entire galaxies with their light. Although they were initially assumed to be very distant stars, but further research has proven that false. The brightness of a quasar is a stark contrast to the effectively invisible supermassive black holes that power them. A quasar is essentially a supermassive black hole that is feeding.

Any matter or light which falls within the event horizon of a black hole falls into the black hole and cannot escape. Quasars, or quasi-stellar radio sources, are formed when particles near the edges of the black hole are ejected away from the black hole in streams called jets that move outward for millions of light years above and below the supermassive black hole. These particles are accelerated at speeds near the speed of light, which causes them to emit massive amounts of energy and light. This is the reason that quasars shine so brightly.

Since quasars are powered by supermassive black holes it is theoretically possible for any galaxy with a supermassive black hole at its center to contain a quasar. The Milky Way does not have one at its center because there are no materials close enough to fuel one. Astronomers believe that there may once have been one at the center of this galaxy, but that it stopped when fuel ran out. It's possible that if a new source of fuel is introduced (as would happen if the Milky Way were to collide with another galaxy as it is predicted to do in 4 billion years) the Milky Way would once again contain a quasar.

Pulsar

Pulsars are formed by rapidly rotating neutron stars that give off intense amounts of electromagnetic radiation. The first pulsars were discovered in 1967 as scientists noticed quick bursts of radiation emitting from a certain point in the sky. These pulses are what the pulsar got its name from. Although they were originally viewed in the radio spectrum of electromagnetic radiation, pulsars can also be observed using optical, x-ray, and gamma ray methods.

When a large star reaches the end of its life cycle it will detonate in a supernova with enough force to crush the protons and electrons at the core into neutrons. This is what creates a neutron star. As these tremendous forces cause the star to begin collapsing inward it will maintain its same angular momentum. Therefore, as it decreases in size, it's rotational speed increases proportionally. This allows neutron stars to rotate generate powerful magnetic fields and rotate incredibly quickly. Some pulsars (rotating neutron stars) have been known to rotate up to hundreds of times each second.

The intense magnetic field of these pulsars generates a beam of light that radiates outwards from the star. These beams are what cause the appearance that the pulsar is giving off regular pulses of light. Pulsars spin at such regular rates that they can even be used by astronomers as a form of spatial timer. Some pulsars also have planets in orbit around them – although they don't create very hospitable environments.

Over periods of tens to hundreds of millions of years, the original energy of the pulsar will fade, its rotational speed will slow, and the beams of light will be extinguished.

Binary Systems

Looking at the night sky from the perspective of Earth the night sky appears to be filled with a countess number of individual stars. In reality the majority of the "single" bright spots of light are actually systems of multiple stars – other solar systems, entire galaxies, and most commonly binary systems. A binary system is a pair of two stars that orbit about each other around a center point between them. The brighter of the two stars is called the primary star, and the dimmer of the two stars is called the secondary star. Several types of binary systems have been discovered, and some of the more common classifications include those of close binaries, wide binaries, visual binaries, spectroscopic binaries, and astrometric binaries.

Wide binaries are systems in which the two stars are very distant from each other. Sometimes they are even distant enough from each other to be observed through optical telescopes. In systems such as this each star will have very little influence on its pair other than holding it in orbit.

In contrast, close binaries are systems in which the two stars are close enough to each other that they do have an influence on the other's development. Often in a close binary system the primary (or larger) star will pull mass and materials from the secondary (or smaller) star allowing it to grow more massive. In some cases the pull of the primary star is strong enough to completely envelop the smaller star in the pair.

Visual binaries are systems that are wide enough to be seen visually. Only a small percentage of binary systems are visual binaries – around 5%. More often than not, binary systems must be studied and identified using other methods. Spectroscopic binaries are one example of this. These are binary systems that can only be observed through studies of their spectroscopic properties (such as red shift and blue shift). By examining the properties of light that the system emits, astronomers can determine information about the binary system.

Lastly, astrometric binaries are systems in which only one of the stars can be identified, but based on its movement on other properties astronomers can infer that it must be in a binary pairing. This could be a result of the primary star simply outshining the dimmer secondary star, the secondary star remaining eclipsed behind the primary star, the secondary star being too dim to be seen for Earth, or even simply that further observation is necessary to find the star.

Comets

In many ways, comets are similar to asteroids. Comets are astronomical bodies that are typically less than ten miles (16 kilometers) in diameter. They are small bodies composed primarily of ice and dust – lending to their nickname as "dirty snowballs." The main components of comets are fairly similar to those of the ice giants Neptune and Uranus, with frozen water, ammonia, carbon dioxide, and methane all being found commonly in their cores. Astronomers suspect that comets may be fragments left over from the creation of the solar system. They may even have been the first sources of organic material on the planet Earth.

Comets and asteroids differ in the fact that comets possess a coma and a tail. A coma is a gaseous cloud that emerges around a comet as it passes closely to the Sun. The heat from the Sun melts and evaporates some of the frozen interior of the comet, creating the coma. In some comets, the coma can extend for as much as 1 million miles (1.6 million kilometers) out from the center of the comet. Essentially the coma is a form of atmosphere that is very thin and extends far into space around the comet.

The second distinguishing aspect of comets is their tails. Comets actually have two tails that stream behind them – a dust tail and a gas tail. As with the coma, the tails of the comet are formed as a result of interactions with solar radiation and winds. As the heat from the Sun causes materials within the comet to vaporize many are left behind and appear as tails. The two tails tend to have slightly different directions. The dust tail often appears to have a slight curve, whereas the gas tail is always facing directly away from the Sun. This is a result of solar winds which have a more powerful effect on the light, gaseous ions of the gas tail than they do on the dust tail.

Tails extend even further into space than the coma does, extending up to 100 million miles behind the comet. The coma and the tails of gas and dust are what give comets their brilliant appearance. As the ice and dust reflect light from the Sun, they appear to glow.

Like many bodies in the solar system, most comets are bound in an orbit about the Sun. They are simply more distant in their orbits than the majority of the planets. Comets are classified as short-period comets, which have an orbit time of less than 200 years, long-period comets, with an orbit time of longer than 200 years, and single-apparition (or hyperbolic comets) which are not bound to the Sun, and only pass by it once. Short period comets are believed to originate from the Kuiper belt. The Kuiper belt is a disc of icy materials outside the orbit of Neptune. They are pulled inwards by gravitational forces by planets and begin eventually begin moving inwards closer to the Sun.

Long period comets are believed to original from the Oort belt. This is a spherical cloud of icy materials from outside the Kuiper belt. It extends all the way from the Kuiper belt halfway to the next nearest star to the Sun – Alpha Centauri – which is over 90 million light years away. It is difficult to know the origin of single-apparition comets because they are not bound to the Sun, and their orbital paths lead them out of the solar system.

Blackbodies

An important factor in the study of stars is the knowledge that color and temperature are correlated to each other. This knowledge is built off of an understanding of the concept of blackbodies and blackbody radiation. A blackbody is an idealized object that will absorb radiation at all levels in the electromagnetic spectrum. This means that no light shining on a blackbody will be reflected, and none will pass through it. As a result, the body would appear black –which is where the term blackbody originates.

Blackbodies do not necessarily appear black, however, because a perfect blackbody will also display the unique characteristic of emitting light at all spectrums. No object yet discovered is a perfect blackbody. Essentially, an object can be considered a black body if the radiation that it emits is a result of its temperature. Because of this solid objects and stars are close approximates to one, so the principles relating to blackbody radiation are often applied to them.

Blackbodies emit radiation in very specific ways. Max Planck was a German scientist who is famous for studying the emissions of blackbodies. Planck was able to create a formula that would relate the wavelength and intensity of blackbody radiation. When graphed, this equation appears as a curve which peaks at a unique wavelength determined by the temperature of the object.

The significance of Planck's work is that it means that at a particular temperature every blackbody will emit light according to the same pattern, regardless of its composition. Therefore, measuring spectral patterns will allow scientists to determine the temperatures of distant stars. His work relating to blackbody radiation also became the foundation for quantum mechanics, opening a whole new field of physics for study.

OTHER GALAXIES AND GALAXY CLUSTERS

While the Milky Way Galaxy is of importance as the galaxy in which the Earth is located, it is only a small part of the larger universe, which contains several different forms of galaxies. Galaxies are generally characterized by their structure. The three galaxy structures are spiral galaxies, elliptical galaxies and irregular galaxies. In addition to these three forms of galaxies, astronomers will often refer to radio galaxies. Rather than being a specific type of galaxy with its own form and structure, radio galaxy is a term used to indicate a galaxy that emits large amounts of radiation in the radio frequency.

TYPES OF GALAXIES

Spiral Galaxies

The most famous type of galaxy is a spiral galaxy – the galaxy class to which the Milky Way belongs. The structure of a spiral galaxy has the general appearance of a twisting spiral, making it one of the more dynamic and visually appealing forms of galaxies. Spiral galaxies are typically younger and shine brighter than other galaxy structures. They include three main components: a bulge, a disk, and a halo. The oldest part of the galaxy is the bulge at the center. Here, older stars are clumped together in irregular orbits around a supermassive black hole. Not all spiral galaxies contain this bulge, but many of them do.

The disc is the more characteristic part of the spiral galaxy. Spiral galaxies have a flat disc of orbiting materials that take the shape of arms spiraling outwards from the bulge. The Milky Way is a bar-spiral galaxy with four arms. The Sun is located on the outer edge of one of these arms, making it very distant from the center of the galaxy.

Some spiral galaxies have multiple arms, while others have only two. Still others have a bar shape that crosses the center, and arms which spiral outwards from there. 60 percent of spiral galaxies have multiple sets of arms. 30 percent have only two arms, and the remaining 10 percent have faded to a point where their arms are not well-defined enough to pick out. This is not surprising because it is believed that spiral galaxies eventually morph into elliptical galaxies as star formation slows and the spirals of the galaxy tight and contract.

Spiral galaxies also contain a halo of stars that surround the bulge above and below the main disc section. This is a loose spherical section of stars that likely develop in the galaxy's early stages (rarely does significant star formation occur anywhere other than in the disc).

Elliptical Galaxies

Elliptical galaxies are essentially shaped like and elongated sphere. This means that to an observer an elliptical galaxy would simply appear like a two-dimensional disc of light- brightest in the center, and fading farther out from it. The galaxies aren't simply a large bright spot, of course. The appearance is caused by groupings of stars that are focused around the center point, and then decreases on the outskirts of the galaxies.

Whereas spiral galaxies have a flattened, disk-like shape, elliptical galaxies tend to be more three dimensional. Because they are elliptical, their exact shape and size can be obscured based on their position relative to the Earth, but they are generally classified based on how elliptical their shape is. A classification of E0 indicates a galaxy that is nearly perfectly circular, and the higher the classification is, the more elliptical the galaxy appears.

In addition to being less visually exciting than spiral galaxies, elliptical galaxies are generally older and dimmer. This makes them more difficult to identify and classify than other forms of galaxies are. Because they are brighter and easier to see, scientists have identified more spiral galaxies than they have elliptical galaxies. However, astronomers believe that there are a greater number of elliptical galaxies in the universe than there are spiral galaxies – they just can't be as easily observed because of their relative dimness.

The range of sizes in elliptical galaxies is vast. On the smaller end, elliptical galaxies have been identified that are 10 times smaller than the Milky Way Galaxy. Conversely, some of the largest galaxies in the universe, including one recently identified as being 50 times larger than the Milky Way with 2000 times the mass, are elliptical galaxies.

Elliptical galaxies are likely formed by the collisions of two or more spiral galaxies. The violet collision causes them to lose their shapes and morph into the more loosely structured elliptical galaxies. This would also explain why elliptical galaxies are generally much older than spiral galaxies are.

Irregular Galaxies

Irregular Galaxies are a unique type of galaxy that does not fit into the classifications of any other type of galaxy. About 3% of galaxies that have been discovered are irregular galaxies that don't have any sort of identifiable shape. Some irregular galaxies are formed by partial collisions with other galaxies, and others are formed as irregularly shaped stellar clouds form many new stars in a very short period of time, but there is no single cause behind the anomalous structures of these galaxies.

There are two basic types of irregular galaxies. Type I Irregular galaxies are the more structured of the two. They may develop arms or bulges as spiral galaxies do, but they never achieve the level of organization of a true spiral galaxy. The bulges are generally not located at the center of the galaxy, with a random placement of stars and other features. Type II Irregular galaxies are even less structured. They are composed of large amounts of gas and dust that are difficult to see through. Although they shine fairly brightly, it is difficult to distinguish individual stars and features within them.

Radio Galaxies

Radio galaxies emit thousands to millions of times more radio waves than other galaxies. The most likely source of these emissions is a form of low luminosity quasar.

This means that there is a supermassive black hole at the center of the galaxy that causes radio emissions. Because radio emissions are very difficult to see, many inferences have to be made about the characteristics of radio galaxies.

COSMIC DISTANCES

One of the challenges faced by astronomers is determining distances of various astronomical objects. Distances in space are so vast that they cannot be considered in the same terms that they are on Earth, or even as they are within the solar system. For example, the next closest star to our Sun is the star Alpha Centauri. Even being the closest star to the Sun, Alpha Centauri is so far away that the light that it emits must travel for more than four years to reach the Earth. Light travels at a speed of approximately 300 million meters per second, which means that the total distance between these two stars is more than 25,000,000,000,000 miles (more than 40,000,000,000,000 kilometers).

Clearly different units are needed in order to better understand cosmic distances. Common astronomical terms used as measures include light years (the distance light travels in a year which is approximately 6 trillion miles), parsecs (which are approximately 3.2 light years), and astronomical units (the distance between the Earth and the Sun, abbreviated as AU).

In addition to the use of more appropriate terms, astronomers are also challenged in finding ways to measure the distance astronomical objects are from the Earth. Combinations of information about magnitude, mass, luminosity, chemical compositions and other features are all used in determining clues about an objects distance. In addition to these tools, astronomer's use a class of astronomical objects that are known as standard candles in order to determine astronomical distances.

A standard candle is essentially any object with a known absolute magnitude. If the absolute magnitude of the object can be determined, then it is possible to calculate its apparent magnitude. Because the two measures are related proportionally by their distance, once both are known then the absolute distance of the object can also be calculated. The two most common examples of standard candles are Cepheid variable stars and Type I supernovae.

Cepheid variable stars are stars that have been discovered to have a regularly changing apparent magnitude. In other words, the stars grow dimmer and brighter at regular intervals. The period of a Cepheid will typically range anywhere from 1 to 70 days. What makes them really valuable as standard candles is that their period is directly proportional to their absolute magnitude. The greater the star's period, then the greater its absolute magnitude is.

The other factor that makes Cepheid variables use as standard candles is that they are fairly common. Cepheids are commonly found in groupings of population I stars in the spiral disc of spiral galaxies. This means that when a Cepheid is identified in a distant galaxy, the distance to that galaxy can easily be determine once the period of the star has been measured.

Type I Supernovae are also important standard candles because they are believed to all have the same absolute luminosity. This means that once a supernovae has been observed, then astronomers are able to calculate the distance to its location. Assuming that it is correct that each supernovae has the same luminosity, these calculations should be accurate within 5%.

 The Universe: Contents, Structure and Evolution

LARGE-SCALE STRUCTURE

THE LOCAL GROUP

The universe spans an unimaginably vast area. While scientists continue in the search to understand its exact shape, size, and composition, there is necessarily a lot of reliance on theory, assumption, and inference when discussing its large scale structure. Starting small, however, we can begin with what is known about the area immediately surrounding our own viewpoint from the Earth.

The area within 5 million light years of the center of the Milky Way is known as the Local Group. The Local Group is a small unit of around 50 galaxies which are bound together by a mutual gravitational attraction. About half of the galaxies are elliptical, with the remaining half being a mixture of irregular and spiral types.

Many of these galaxies are even larger than the Milky Way. It's likely that there are even more that are simply too faint to have been identified yet. The number is also regularly challenging as galaxies combine, or are consumed by other galaxies. In fact, the Milky Way is currently in the process of incorporating a small galaxy nearby, and it's likely that it has consumed other galaxies in the past.

The largest galaxies within the Local Group are the Milky Way, Andromeda, and Triangulum Galaxies. Each of these three is a spiral galaxy, and has additional small galaxies that act as satellite galaxies. The Andromeda Galaxy is a particularly helpful reference point for astronomers. It is a barred spiral galaxy, similar to the Milky Way. It is far enough away that the entire galaxy can be examined, but close enough that individual stars can also identified and studied. Studying the Andromeda Galaxy reveals important information and clues as to the structure of the Milky Way as well.

Superclusters, Filaments, Sheets, and Voids

Just as the galaxies of the Local Group tend to cluster together, a pattern of grouping seems to extend throughout the universe. This gives rise to large-scale structural features known as superclusters, filaments, sheets, and voids. The natural grouping pattern of galaxies and stars provides evidence that the universe is not evenly distributed. This is a significant claim because it means that in order for these large scale structures to have formed, the early universe must not have been uniformly dense either.

Each smaller formation is part of another larger formation, with the pattern continuing and spanning throughout the observable universe. This process is known as hierarchical clustering. This refers to the pattern of many smaller objects merging again and again to form larger structures.

Galaxies are the basic unit of large-scale structures. Galaxies form groups and clusters, which in turn form superclusters. Superclusters are formed by combinations of many smaller galaxy clusters. The Milky Way itself is expected to merge with the Andromeda Galaxy – the next largest galaxy in the Local Group. Eventually the entire Local Group with merge with a larger cluster called the Virgo cluster. Even known all of these structures are being pull in towards other nearby superclusters with which they will eventually merge. These superclusters – the Centaurus and Shapley superclusters – have been nicknamed the Great Attractor because of the great force that they exert on the surrounding areas of the universe.

Filaments are another of the largest scale structures in the universe. Filaments are long threadlike structures where dense populations of superclusters gather together. Filaments can extend for hundreds of millions of lights years, with thicknesses of only several million light years.

Another large-scale structure is called a galactic sheet, sometimes known as a galactic wall or great wall. These structures are similar to filaments in that they are large, dense groupings of clusters and superclusters. The difference between the two is that galactic sheets appear to fan out in a honeycomb shape, rather than remaining in a single thread. Galactic sheets span hundreds of millions of light years in length and width, but with thicknesses of only 20 million light years.

As galaxies cluster into sheets and filaments of densely populated areas, they necessarily leave behind vast stretches of space that are very thinly populated. These spans of relatively empty space are known as voids. In cases where the void is very extensive they are called super voids. Voids are not necessarily entirely empty of galaxies.

Extended observation has shown that a few galaxies do exist in these regions of space. In fact, the galaxies that remain within voids often form their own very small, thin filaments within the void. The difference is that galaxies are just far more spread out, and are generally dimmer within the voids.

SIZE OF THE UNIVERSE

The universe is defined as all existing matter and space, sometimes known as the cosmos. Everything from the Earth to the Milky Way Galaxy, to the farthest reaches that can be observed with today's technology and beyond constitutes the universe.

Determining the size of the universe is a difficult task for astronomers. Part of the reason for this is simply the limitations of the speed of light. Although light is the fastest moving thing known to man, its speed is still insignificant when compared with the enormity of the universe. Scientists can only observe an object once its light reaches the Earth. This means that looking at the night sky is really like looking into the past – you see the stars as they were when the light left them, not as they are. For example, the Sun is eight light minutes away from Earth. This means that at any given moment, the light that shines down on a person actually left the Sun eight minutes prior. If the Sun were to disappear, observers on Earth wouldn't know it for eight minutes!

Eight minutes isn't a very long time, but as objects become further and further away the time difference between what is observed and what is currently occurring becomes even greater. The next closest star to the Sun is Alpha Centauri which is slightly more than four light years away. This means that all observations that scientists make about the star are actually based on events that occurred four years ago.

Expanding even further beyond this, much of the phenomenon that scientists currently study exist so far away that they could predate even the Earth. This makes our view of the universe from Earth very distorted by the limitations of time, with some objects appearing as they were only short time ago, while others appear as they did so long ago that the information is likely no longer accurate or relevant.

Another factor which makes determining the precise size of the universe is the fact that most astronomers agree that the universe is expanding. Because of this expansion, when light from distant parts of the universe reach the Earth, the objects that they display will be even further away than they were originally.

This is where the concept of Doppler shifts becomes important in measuring distances. By determining the severity with which distance objects are red-shifted relative to Earth, it can be determined the distance they have traveled in the meantime. Using this information we know that the observable universe has a radius of 46 billion light years.

There is an important distinction between the observable universe and the universe, though. The observable universe is the portion of the universe that we have been able to examine. This is mapped out in a 92 billion light year sphere extending with the Earth around the center. Because it isn't yet possible to see light any more distant than this, it's probable that more exists beyond this plane that simply hasn't been observed. Further, the universe will continue to expand as more distant information is collected as well.

SHAPE OF THE UNIVERSE

For the same reason that it is difficult to determine the size of the universe, the shape of the universe is similarly difficult to determine. An important aspect of this question is whether the size of the universe is finite or infinite. If the size of the universe is finite, then both its size and its shape can eventually be precisely determined. However, if it is infinite then neither can be precisely determined.

Einstein's theories of relativity offer some answers to the question of the shape of the universe. He argued that mass has the ability to alter the shape of space and time. This indicates that the amount of mass in the universe, and its density, are responsible in determining what eventual shape the universe will take. Scientists have determined the critical density of the universe at which current expansion would stop. Whether the actual density is greater than, less than, or equal to this quantity is the matter in question.

If the actual density is greater than the critical density, then it contains sufficient mass to eventually overcome the expansionary forces and the universe will come to rest at a finite size and spherical shape. This is the only outcome that would potentially result in a finite universe, also called a closed universe. Although the bounds of the universe would be finite, they would be impossible to detect – a particle at any given starting place would eventually end up right back where it started if it just continued traveling.

There are some concerns with this possibility. Firstly, if this were the case, then once the universe stopped expanding it would necessarily begin to contract under the gravitational forces of the various galaxies and astronomical phenomenon contained within it. This would cause a reversal of the expansion and pull the universe back into a tiny space – an event nicknamed the "Big Crunch." However, calculations indicate that the universe will not stop expanding, so this theory is typically discarded.

The second possibility is that the actual density could be less than the critical density of the universe. If this were the case the mass contained within the universe would not be sufficient to stop its expansion. It would simply continue expanding indefinitely. This would cause what is called a "negative curve" to the universe. Its shape would be like a saddle, or a sheet of paper arched upwards. Because of its infinitely expanding size, this model is categorized as an open universe.

The final option is that the actual density of the universe exactly matches the critical density. If this is the case, then the expansion of the universe will be slowed down gradually over an infinite amount of time. In other words, the amount of mass in the universe is exactly the amount that will stop it from expanding after an infinite amount of time. But, as time progresses, the amount of its expansion will slow.

In the scenario where actual density and critical density are equal, the universe must be flat and of infinite size. Based on the most recent calculations, it has been concluded with only a .4% margin of error that the universe is flat, making this the most correct of the three proposed models.

A flat universe can be a difficult concept to understand. It's important to remember that each of these three shapes – sphere, saddle, and flat – are two or three dimensional representations being used to describe the four dimensional universe. When scientists say that the universe is "flat" it does not necessarily mean that the universe is shaped like an infinitely large piece of paper. In fact, observable space continues outward in all dimensions from the Earth as far as it is currently possible to see.

What is determined by the curvature of the universe is what geometric rules apply to space. Because the universe is "flat," we know that two particles moving in parallel lines will never intersect or diverge. They will simply continue moving infinitely through space. Also, Pythagorean mathematics can be applied to the stars because all triangles will have angles summing to 180 degrees.

Contrast this with the geometric properties of a spherical, closed universe. The positive curvature of the universe would have the result that parallel lines would eventually intersect, and the three angles of a triangle would have a sum greater than 180 degrees. Alternatively, in a negatively curved universe parallel lines would continuously diverge from one another, never intersecting but moving continuously further apart. This would cause triangles to have angles summing to less than 180 degrees. Therefore, the significance of a flat universe is that we know that the universe expands in a geometrically consistent way, whatever size it ultimately comes to in its infinite expansion.

COMPOSITION OF THE UNIVERSE

The Earth is a terrestrial planet, making heavier elements and metals very common in daily experience. However, while the presents of heavier elements such as oxygen, iron, and nickel are found very commonly here, they are actually incredibly rare throughout the universe as a whole. The vast majority of the universe is composed of much lighter elements. Hydrogen and Helium dominate the spectrum, with Hydrogen accounting for 73% of the elements in the universe, and Helium accounting for another 25% approximately. This means that heavier elements that make the building blocks of life on Earth – oxygen, carbon, nitrogen, etc. – compose only a fraction of a percent of the universe.

The current ratio of Hydrogen and Helium developed over a process of time. In fact, at the time of the creation of the universe, Hydrogen was actually much more abundant than it is currently. It is expected that shortly after creation, the proportions were closer to 92% Hydrogen and 8% Helium. Heavier metals have slowly come into existence over billions of years through the process of star formation and extinction. Recall that the primary source of energy within stars is the nuclear fusion of Hydrogen into Helium. This is why over the past several billion years the proportion of Helium has increased relative to Hydrogen – it is being transformed as energy is released within stars.

This is similarly how heavier "metal" elements have been introduced into the universe. Recall that the ending phases of a stars life cycle involve further fusion of Helium into denser elements, and intense amounts of pressure and heat that can facilitate it. Very slowly over time the metallic terrestrial elements that are so common on Earth were formed within stars and eventually recombined into new systems. This is why such elements are so rare throughout the universe- it takes extreme amounts of heat, pressure, and time in order for them to form.

DARK MATTER AND DARK ENERGY

Understanding the composition of the universe goes beyond simply discoveries about its chemical composition. As scientists have studied the structure and composition of the universe it has become increasingly that there are energies and matter at work that exist outside the realm of our own elemental system. In fact, the groupings of protons, neutrons, and electrons – known as baryonic matter – that form the basis of scientific thought are now thought to compose only 5% of the total matter and energy in the universe. The remaining 95% takes the form of dark matter and dark energy.

Scientists first began to suspect the existence of dark matter as they studied distant galaxy clusters in the 1930s. After studying the mass and movements of the various galaxies in the Coma cluster, it became clear that either the mass of the galaxies must be far greater than that of the luminous (visible) materials, or that the galaxies should have easily overcome each other's gravitational pull and escaped into deep space long ago.

This belief was furthered as it became apparent that not only were the larger galaxy clusters mysteriously lower than expected in their total mass, but individual galaxies are as well. Stars on the outer part of galaxies near ours move at speeds that should allow them to escape the gravitational pull of the galaxy, yet they remain in motion as they are, circling around the outer edges of the galaxy.

The third evidence of the existence of dark matter is gravitational lensing - a phenomenon explained by Einstein's theories. Einstein's theories showed that large gravitational forces have the ability to actually bend space. This causes light that moves over these areas to curve around the massive object as it travels through the curved areas of space. This is called gravitational lensing, and it occurs around dark matter. As light travels through space and approaches an area filled with dark matter, it will curve around that matter and continue on. From the perspective of Earth it will appear as though there is a circle of light around empty space. This "empty space" is really dark matter.

A task even more difficult than identifying the presence of dark matter is to understand what it actually is. Dark matter composes 27% of the observable universe, and yet very little is known about what it is, and how it functions. As far as scientists can tell, dark mater does not interact with the electromagnetic world. This means that it does not absorb, reflect, or emit light. This is why it is called dark matter. Since it doesn't interact with light, there is no way for it to be observed.

In addition to not interacting with light, it seems that dark matter is not composed of the same types of particles (protons, neutrons, and electrons) as baryonic matter. The only way that dark matter interacts with the baryonic matter that composes 5% of the universe is through gravitational forces. This doesn't mean that the composition of dark matter will not one day emerge. Scientists have several theories about what composes dark matter – the most prominent of which is WIMPs – Weakly Interacting Massive Particles. These are tiny particles that react very weakly with baryonic matter through gravity.

Not all of the universe can be accounted for with these two quantities. The combined amounts of baryonic matter and dark matter still only account for 32 percent of the universe. Recall that based on general relativity, mass and energy are interchangeable quantities. The remaining 68 percent of the universe can therefore be attributed to dark energy. Dark energy is a form of energy that exists in the vacuum of space, and is evenly distributed throughout both space and time.

Dark energy is an important concept because it completes the explanation as to why the universe is expanding. Theories such as the Big Bang account for the expansion of the universe, but it would also lead to the ultimate conclusion that that expansion must eventually slow and stop under the gravitational forces at work within planets, stars, and galaxies. However, the study of early galaxies has shown that the rate of expansion of the universe is actually increasing with time. This means that there must be some form of energy that acts against natural gravitational forces in the universe.

This unknown form of energy is called dark energy. There are two main theories that attempt to describe what dark energy is. Some argue that dark energy is an actual substance that – although we cannot yet detect it - fills the void of space. This substance is sometimes called "quintessence" and essentially operates as an "antigravity" force, pushing against the universe instead of pulling it back together.

A more popular explanation for dark energy is that it is simply a numeric property of space. Before it was known that the universe was expanding, Einstein's theories required an additional figure to reconcile them with the steady-state universe theory. As the equations were written, the universe would have to be either expanding or contracting, so he calculated the value of a cosmological constant. Once it had been proven that the universe was in fact expanding, Einstein dropped the cosmological constant from the equations, calling it his greatest blunder. However, this concept of a cosmological constant fits with the expansion of space due to dark energy. The problem is explaining why it exists, and proving why it holds the value that it does.

Another possibility is that Einstein's theories are simply incorrect about the properties of gravity. However, to this point all attempts to improve his theories have been unsuccessful. More often equations that explain the motions otherwise attributed to dark matter and energy, simply cause a break-down of all other gravitational interactions. So for now, the theories about dark matter and dark energy stand.

THE BIG BANG

Currently the most widely accepted theory for the origins of the universe is the Big Bang. This theory argues for a finite beginning point in time in which the universe came into existence. This beginning point would to set at 13.7 billion years ago in a violet period of expansion, heating, and cooling. While the Big Bang theory can explain how the universe came into existence, where matter, space, and time originate, and so forth, it is difficult, if not impossible, to determine what caused it to occur in the first place.

Trying to understand what happened before the Big Bang is like trying to determine what is south of the South Pole. Just as there is no defined "south" beyond the South Pole, there is no defined time before the Big Bang. Remember that space, time, mass, and energy are all linked quantities. Without the existence of space, time cannot be considered either. Therefore, all of these things came into existence at one single point in time – called the singularity – for reasons that cannot be explained with present understandings and applications of physical and natural laws.

Our understanding about the events of the Big Bang begins right after this moment where expansion started – approximately 10-43 seconds afterwards. Here is where the universe began rapidly expanding into existence. A common misconception about the Big Bang is that it was an explosion. In reality, it was an expansion. Particles double in size nearly 100 times in span of time covering only a small fraction of a second. Growth this dramatic requires that space expanded at speeds exceeding even the speed of light.

By the time a full second passed, the majority of the particles that form the building blocks of baryonic matter had come into existence. This includes quarks, electrons, protons, neutrons, anti-electrons, photons and other more exotic types of particles as well. All of the existing matter, however, is so intensely heated that atoms are unable to form, with the temperature of the universe rapidly cooling from several quadrillion degrees to 1 trillion degrees.

For the next three minutes after this first second, various types of particles collide, annihilating each other and creating other forms of particles. By the time three minutes pass, the universe cooled further to a point where nucleosynthesis became possible – around 1 billion degrees. In this phase of nucleosynthesis, protons and neutrons combine through nuclear fusion, and the simple elements that compose the majority of the universe emerged – hydrogen, helium, and trace amounts of lithium.

While 1 billion degrees is much cooler than the universe was in its first few seconds of existence, it is still too hot for nuclei to effectively capture electrons. As a result, as cooling slowed to a much more gradual pace, the universe remained in a state called the photon epic for nearly 400,000 years. In the photon epic, the universe was filled with elements in an effective plasma state, with free floating electrons in a very hot cloud of nuclei. This is also known as the primordial fireball. It isn't possible for this early time to be observed because photons could not travel through this medium. The earliest visible time in the universe occurs as the end of this stage in a phase known as recombination. This is the phase of the universe that is visible through Cosmic Microwave Background radiation.

During the recombination era the temperature of the universe cooled far enough that electrons could bind to the ionized helium and hydrogen atoms. This placed them in a stable state, and allowed, for the first time, the flowing of photons (i.e. light entered existence). Although light would have been capable of transmitting after this point, the next 150 million years are generally considered the Dark Age of the universe because no stars had yet formed, meaning that there were no stars to create energy and light.

Over the next 13.7 billion years leading up to today, stars, black holes, galaxies, and solar systems gradually came into existence, until reaching the point that we are in today. Our solar system entered existence approximately 8.5 billion years after the Big Bang. This was all made possible due to the smallest of fluctuations in density in the early matter of the otherwise homogenous universe.

ALTERNATIVE ORIGIN THEORIES

The two most popular theories that stand in contrast to the Big Bang are the steady-state theory, and the expansion and contraction theory. The steady-state theory was an early rival theory about the universe. The main assertions of the steady-state theory are that the universe is essentially the same in all places at all times. In other words, it has continued in this steady state for an infinite amount of time, with no beginning and no foreseeable end.

This theory worked reasonably well as an explanation when it was first proposed, but as further information about the universe was discovered, it became less and less likely. For example, as telescopes allowed scientists to see further and further into space, it became increasingly clear that the universe evolves over time. Seeing distant quasars, black holes, and galaxies made it clear that although the evolutionary time scale is incredibly long, evolution does occur, meaning that a further explanation was necessary.

A second flaw to the steady state universe theory is that it defies the Second Law of Thermodynamics. This law state that the amount of disorder in the universe increases with time. Therefore, the universe could not logically remain in a steady state indefinitely. Rather, it would have to move towards a higher state of entropy, causing the galaxy to ultimately degrade and life to collapse.

The discovery of Cosmic Microwave Radiation further disproved the viability of a steady-state universe. The theory could offer no explanation for why this background radiation would exist throughout the universe, whereas it is effectively predicted by the theory of the Big Bang. With time, the steady state theory has been mostly rejected.

A second theory is the expansion and contraction theory, sometimes known as the oscillation theory. This theory is more of an extension to the Big Bang than it is a contradiction, although there are some important distinctions between the two. The theory of expansion and contraction agrees that the universe has been expanding from a denser state for several billion years, but it furthers the theory. This theory predicts that at some point in the future the expansion of the universe will reverse course. The result will be that the universe will again contract itself into a single point as it was before the Big Bang.

As the universe compresses itself back towards a single point as it was before the Big Bang energy and forces will build up within the matter and cause it to rebound and expand again. In other words, the oscillation theory argues that the universe does not have a single start point. Rather it has been following a pattern of expansion and contraction repeated for an indeterminable amount of time.

This is one important way in which this differs from the theory of the Big Bang. By stating that patterns of expansion and contraction happened in the past and will continue in the future, it rejects the idea of a single finite beginning to the universe. That is an important concept within the Big Bang.

Another way in which the oscillation theory differs from the Big Bang is that it argues against the concept of a singularity, or single point of origin. This is one of the most contested concepts of the Big Bang, because a singularity would require the existence of a point with infinite energy, and yet no mass. The oscillation theory solves this by arguing that the early expansion of the universe happened at a much slower rate, and that the matter was originally much less condensed than it would be if a singularity existed.

Life in the Universe

EXTREMES OF LIFE ON EARTH

Earth is a relatively young planet, orbiting about a relatively young star of average size. Despite this, it is the only planet confirmed to have an abundance of life. Not only is there life on Earth, but it has been present in some form for nearly all of Earth's existence, and the variety of life is nothing short of astounding.

On this single planet there are countless forms of aquatic life. Some capable of surviving the harshest deep-ocean pressures, heat, and environments, and some living close to the surface and taking occasional ventures up for air. In contrast to these water-dependent creates, the opposite also exits, with a variety of desert organisms that can survive with almost no water, including plant forms, small animals, and microbes. Some bacteria thrive in environments toxic to humans, such as liquid nitrogen, or Sulphur springs, while others are even more fragile than humans. There are insects with hundreds of legs, and snakes that maintain mobility despite having no limbs. While some forms of life have life spans of less than a day, others seem to be nearly immortal.

The longer that life is studied, the more varied and dynamic it proves to be. Yet the question of the origin of life on Earth is nearly as elusive as the creation of the universe itself. Research and classification have been important tool in tracing the development of life since the early history of the Earth. A probable Last Common Ancestor to all organisms on Earth. The remaining question is to how the original organisms developed. There are two leading theories about this: chemical development and panspermia. The essential difference between the two theories is as to whether life has Earthly origins or otherwise.

One theory of the development of life on Earth is panspermia. This theory credits extraterrestrial origins with the formation of life. The basis of the theory suggests that the earliest organic compounds must have formed on another planet in the universe and was somehow transported to the Earth through early meteorite impacts.

The benefit of this theory is that is explains how such complex molecules as DNA came to exist on the Earth. It also explains how life came to exist so quickly – as life arose only a short time after the creation of the Earth itself. However, it cannot give explanation as to how they would have developed elsewhere either. Furthermore, if organic molecules could be transported through space, it seems likely that life would be much more abundant than it appears to be.

The more popular of the two theories is that of chemical development on the planet Earth. This theory argues that all of the building blocks of life could have been created through reactions that, while not repeatable today, would have been possible based on the Earth's early composition and atmospheric properties. Part of the trouble with theories about the chemical development of life on Earth is the delicate balance between organic molecules. DNA is the building block of life, and it requires other molecules such as enzymes and proteins, in order to synthesize or reproduce. However, DNA has the coded instructions for how these proteins should be formulated as well.

As a solution to this scientists argue that early forms of life relied instead upon RNA which could have been more easily produced. Only once the more complex molecules required for protein synthesis had developed did DNA take its place as the blueprint of life. This is the most accepted explanation of how life developed on Earth, and laboratory reproductions of the early conditions of the Earth have shown that compounds such as amino acids, sugars, and other organic compounds could have been generated.

These compounds would have formed primarily in warm, oceanic environments creating a loose "soup" of organic compounds. Over time these compounds interacted and developed into early single-celled organisms. These first organisms would have developed 3.8 billion years ago – less a billion years after the origin of the Earth. These single celled organisms would have been able to survive in environments that would be toxic to most life today – the Earth's oceans and continents were still forming, and the atmosphere was nitrogen and methane based, with almost no oxygen.

The next major leap in the evolution of life was the development from single celled organisms to multicellular organisms. For almost 2 billion years single celled life was the only form of life on Earth. This process is explained by the endosymbiotic theory. This theory argues that the specialization of life occurred as mitochondria entered eukaryotic cells. Originally the mitochondria were free-living bacteria, but they entered into a symbiotic relationship with the larger eukaryotic cells that still exists today.

As further symbiotic relationships were entered, cells became increasingly complex. With process of time, life itself became more increasingly complex as well. The development of the first multicellular organisms to the variety of life today happened through a series of simple genetic tweaking over time. Plant life came into existence as eukaryotic cells formed symbiotic relationships with photosynthetic bacteria, allowing chloroplasts to develop and algae and plants to come into existence on dry land.

Within 500 million years of the development of these multicellular, photosynthetic organisms, plant life, fungi, and animals began to develop in their own lines. Over the last 500 million years, fish, then insects, and eventually four legged animals developed. This all eventually lead to the early hominins 6 million years ago, although homo sapiens have only existed for the last 150 thousand years.

LIFE IN THE SOLAR SYSTEM

Although life has not been found anywhere else in the solar system to the extent that it has been found on Earth, there are several locations that are considered strong possibilities for the development of simpler life forms. The four most likely candidates are Jupiter's Moon Europa, Saturn's Moons Enceladus and Titan, and the planet Mars.

Europa

At first glance, Europa is an unlikely candidate for life simply because it is very cold. The entire planet is covered in a layer of ice. However, this icy layer hides liquid water beneath it – a fundamental component in the development of life. Another alluring feature of the Moon is the probability that there is volcanic activity underneath the oceans. These are the same sorts of conditions that likely led to the development of life on Earth, making it a very likely candidate for the development of similar organisms. Subsurface lakes and geysers also provide likely candidates for the formation of life.

Another factor that makes Europa a likely candidate for life is that it has an atmosphere composed of oxygen. While this atmosphere is thin, and doesn't provide much protection from radiation, the surface layer of ice around the Moon does provide protection from solar radiation and other potential dangers. With all this evidence mounting, there are plans for a visit to Europa to investigate further into its potential for developing microbial life.

Mars

The first place that many people think of when the topic of extraterrestrial life emerges is the planet Mars. Although there is not currently any confirmed evidence of life on the planet, evidence indicates that it could more probably have existed there in the past when Mars was a more hospitable place.

Today the planet Mars is plagued by a lack of liquid water, along with a very thin atmosphere that leaves it open to radiation from the Sun and dangerous storms. However, in the past Mars most likely did have a much thicker atmosphere, along with flowing liquid water on its surface that would have allowed for more favorable conditions for life. Ultimately, while Mars is an unlikely candidate for current life, the search continues for any evidence of microbial life during more favorable times in its history.

Enceladus

The next most likely candidate for life in the solar system is a tiny Moon of the planet Saturn named Enceladus. Although the Moon is barely a fraction of the size of the Earth, it contains many of the same encouraging features that have been discovered on Europa. Organic molecules such as carbon, nitrogen, and oxygen have been observed in clouds of water vapor that emerge from within the Moon.

Much like Europa, Enceladus is a very cold place. But the presence of liquid water beneath an icy surface suggests thermal activities occurring within the planet. Like Earth, Enceladus is composed of a rocky mantle providing potential for reactions leading to the formation of organic compounds. Although the small Moon has very little access to warmth from the Sun, its own inward reactions do provide sufficient heat to support microbial life.

Titan

Another of Saturn's Moons, Titan has only recently started to be considered as a possible location for the development of life. The main feature in support of the possibilities is a thick atmosphere which most other Moons and planets lack. Titan was initially rejected as a possible host for life because it is so far from the Sun that it is entirely frozen over, and it doesn't have the underground oceans and lakes that other Moons do. However, recently liquid lakes have been found on Titan's surface – they're just composed of methane rather than water. While any life that potentially developed on Titan would be vastly different from the oxygen dependent life on Earth, scientists are investigating the possibility of methane-based life forms developing on the distant Moon.

LIFE BEYOND THE SOLAR SYSTEM

One of the limiting factors of finding life within this solar system is the amount of time and resources that it takes to investigate the conditions on other bodies within the solar system. This problem increases exponentially as sights are set even broader, and the entirety of the universe is considered along with our small collection of planets. Because of the difficulty of studying other systems and planets, the study of extraterrestrial life is a mixture of some facts, some theories, and some speculation.

An encouraging factor in the search for other life in the universe is the increasing number of habitable areas being discovered. Throughout the universe there are millions of stars with systems of planets in orbit around them, and many of them lie in an area known as the "goldilocks zone" in which liquid water can be maintained on the surface. This alone increases the probability for the development of life.

Despite this, many questions surround the discussion about the possibility of other life, one of which is determining how likely or unlikely the development of life is. Considered from the viewpoint of an outside observer, Earth is a fairly average planet, orbiting a star of average size, and in a system that is relatively young on a universal scale. With billions of stars containing systems that are likely similar to this one, it would seem statistically likely that life would develop elsewhere in the universe just as it did here.

This is known as the Fermi Paradox. Physicist Enrico Fermi noted the overwhelming evidence that life should be able to develop in other regions of space, but was able to find no observable evidence of it. This apparent contradiction continues to plague the search for extraterrestrial life today. This paradox is even further complicated by the realization that because Earth is a relatively young planet, there have been billions of years of opportunities for life to develop and advantage in other areas of the universe, yet there is no evidence of this.

There are several possible explanations to this paradox. Firstly, life may be more unique than scientists have yet suspected. The development of complex molecules like DNA is improbable in random environments. And based on the unfruitful search for life in this solar system, we know that life cannot develop anywhere. The task is determining exactly how improbable it is. Should life develop once for every thousand stars? Or should it develop once for every billion stars? Or could it be that the development of life is so improbable that it really has only happened once in the 13 billion year span of the universe.

Another explanation as to why evidence of life has not yet been found in the universe is that it simply hasn't been found yet. The massive scale of the universe has made it impossible to determine the size and shape of the universe. This leaves the possibility open that there is much that still has to be discovered outside our own observable areas of the universe.

In addition, other forms of life may have developed with an emphasis on different characteristics than it has on Earth. Human beings possess a power for reason and knowledge, but are highly susceptible to disease and injury. Some scientists theorize that life on other planets may develop in single celled forms that are capable of withstanding dramatic astrological phenomenon such as intense radiation, gravitation, or magnetic fields. In any case, there is as yet no evidence of other life beyond the planet Earth. But the simple fact of the vastness and diversity of the universe make it unlikely that no other life exists.

 # Sample Test Questions

1) What major contribution did Aristotle make to today's planetary model?

   A) Planets orbit in ellipses
   B) Earth is round
   C) The Sun is at the center of the solar system
   D) Epicycles

The correct answer is B:) Earth is round. The two major aspects of Aristotle's model were that the Earth is round, and that all of the stars revolved around it. Although his geocentric model was incorrect, he did correctly popularize the notion of the Earth being round.

2) Which of the following was NOT an element of the Ptolemaic model of the solar system?

   A) Epicycles within a planet's orbit
   B) Perfectly circular orbits of planets
   C) Sun-centered model
   D) Existence of an equant

The correct answer is C:) Sun-centered model. Ptolemy maintained a geocentric model of the solar system. However, he did argue that the earth was not directly in the center of the planets' orbits. Rather it was slightly offset at an eccentric point, with a balancing point known as an "equant."

3) Who is credited with constructing the first observatory?

   A) Tycho Brahe
   B) Copernicus
   C) Johannes Kepler
   D) Aristotle

The correct answer is A:) Tycho Brahe. Brahe is credited with building the first dedicated observatory - despite the fact that the telescope had still not been invented he made detailed observations of the motions of several planets that was used by Kepler in his work.

4) Who is known for first using telescopes to observe the stars?

   A) Ptolemy
   B) Copernicus
   C) Brahe
   D) Galileo

The correct answer is D:) Galileo. Although three-powered telescopes were becoming fairly common by this point, Galileo succeeding in constructing a twenty-powered telescope which he used to make his critical observations. His was the first telescope of such magnitude that it could be used for astronomical observations.

5) What was the first type of telescope used?

   A) Seismic
   B) Reflection
   C) Refraction
   D) Radio

The correct answer is C:) Refraction. Galileo's telescopes were refraction telescopes, meaning that they used concave and convex lenses to bend and magnify light.

6) If the optical lens of a refraction telescope has a focal length of 30 inches, and the eyepiece has a focal length of 1.5 inches, what is the telescope's power?

   A) 45
   B) 20
   C) 60
   D) 31.5

The correct answer is B:) 20. Power is calculated as focal length of the optical lens divided by focal length of the eyepiece. In this case 30/1.5=20.

7) Which of the following is NOT an advantage of radio telescopes?

   A) They can measure both visible light and radio waves
   B) Radio telescopes are less affected by poor weather
   C) Hydrogen atoms emit light visible to radio telescopes but not the naked eye
   D) Radio waves travel further through the universe than visible light

The correct answer is A:) They can measure both visible light and radio waves. Radio telescopes pick up radio waves, not visible light.

8) Who is known for mathematically proving the theories of Copernicus and Kepler?

   A) Tycho Brahe
   B) Galileo
   C) Sir Isaac Newton
   D) Ptolemy

The correct answer is C:) Sir Isaac Newton. Newton developed extensive laws of algebra and calculus that proved the validity of Kepler's laws, and Copernicus's model.

COSMIC FORCES

9) Which equation describes Newton's Second Law?

   A) W=Fd
   B) F=ma
   C) v=v0+at
   D) T=Rt

The correct answer is B:) F=ma. Newton's Second Law of Motion describes the behavior of objects for which the net force is not zero. According to Newton, the resulting motion, or acceleration, of an object is proportional to both the force acting on that object, and the mass of the object.

10) The Law of Inertia was developed by which person?

   A) Tycho Brahe
   B) Galileo
   C) Sir Isaac Newton
   D) Johannes Kepler

The correct answer is C:) Sir Isaac Newton. The Law of Inertia is also known as Newton's First Law. It describes the behavior of objects which have no force acting on them.

11) According to the Law of Inertia, an object travelling through space will

   A) Continue in the same manner unless another force acts on it.
   B) Slowly come to rest unless a continuous force is applied.
   C) Sometimes come to rest and sometimes continue in the same manner.
   D) Slow slightly, but not stop completely unless there is friction.

The correct answer is A:) Continue in the same manner unless another force acts on it. Motion is caused by an imbalance of forces, therefore, only additional forces will result in a change in an object's motion.

12) Nuclear fusion works due to the principle of

   A) Mass-energy equivalence
   B) Length contraction
   C) Time dilation
   D) Kepler's Second Law

The correct answer is A:) Mass-energy equivalence. This is possible because as two hydrogen atoms undergo intense collision, one of the protons converts to a neutron. However, the total resulting mass of the particles is decreased in the process. As the total mass of the particles decreases, there is an equivalent release of energy.

13) What is the net force on an object with a mass of 10 kg that moves with an acceleration of 32 m/s2?

   A) 3.2 N
   B) 32 N
   C) 320 N
   D) 3200 N

The correct answer is C:) 320 N. Force = mass x acceleration = 10 * 32 = 320 N.

14) What is the velocity of a 7 kg object moving under a net force of 7 Newtons for 5 seconds?

   A) 7 m/s
   B) 5 m/s
   C) 2 m/s
   D) 1 m/s

The correct answer is B:) 5 m/s. Based on Newton's Second Law a=F/m=7/7= 1 m/s2. Using this acceleration the kinematic equation v=at can be used to determine that the velocity is v=(1)(5)=5m/s.

15) What is the normal force acting on a 20 N object that sits stationary?

   A) 0 N
   B) 5 N
   C) 10 N
   D) 20 N

The correct answer is D:) 20 N. If the force of gravity is pulling on the object with a magnitude of 20 Newtons then based on Newton's Third Law the magnitude of normal force that is required to hold it stationary is also 20 Newtons.

16) Kepler's First Law states that planets orbit in what pattern?

   A) Oval
   B) Circular
   C) Elliptical
   D) Diamond

The correct answer is C:) Elliptical. Kepler was led to the inevitable conclusion that only elliptical orbits would explain the detailed observations that Brahe had made about Mars. For most of the planets in this solar system, the orbits are only slightly elliptical.

17) Kepler's Third Law states that a planet's average distance from the sun is proportional to which of the following?

   A) Its distance from the nearest planet
   B) Its period of orbit
   C) Its diameter
   D) None of the above

The correct answer is B:) Its period of orbit. Kepler's third law states that the square of the period (or time to make a complete orbit) is proportional to the cube of the average distance from the sun. In other words, $T^2 = R^3$ where T is the period of a planet's orbit, and R is the average distance from the sun.

18) The force of gravity on earth is 7.5 times stronger than on Jupiter's moon Europa. How much would a 90 kg object weigh on Europa?

   A) 7.5 kg
   B) 12 kg
   C) 82.5 kg
   D) 675 kg

The correct answer is B:) 12 kg. 90/7.5=12.

19) A box moves 4 meters under a 13 N force. How much work has been done on the box?

   A) .3 Joules
   B) 3.25 Joules
   C) 52 Joules
   D) 208 Joules

The correct answer is C:) 52 Joules. Work=Force x Distance = (13N)(4m)=52 Joules.

20) A force of 5 N acts on a 2 kg box for 3 seconds. What is the Kinetic Energy of the box?

   A) 30 Joules
   B) 41.5 Joules
   C) 56.25 Joules
   D) 63 Joules

The correct answer is C:) 56.25 Joules. Kinetic energy = (1/2)mv2= (1/2)(2)(7.5)2= 56.25 Joules. Velocity can be calculated as F=ma -> a=F/m = 5/2=2.5. v=at=(2.5)(3)=7.5 m/s.

21) What is the gravitational potential energy of a 5 kg box sitting at the top of a 3 meter tall shelf?

   A) 15 Joules
   B) 75 Joules
   C) 105 Joules
   D) 147 Joules

The correct answer is D:) 147 Joules. Gravitational potential energy = mgh = (5)(9.8)(3) = 147 Joules.

22) Kepler's Laws were based on the observations of which astronomer?

   A) Tycho Brahe
   B) Copernicus
   C) Sir Isaac Newton
   D) Galileo

The correct answer is A:) Tycho Brahe. Kepler inherited Brahe's extensive records detailing astronomical observations. He used these to form mathematical conclusions about planetary motion.

23) A 100 kg car accelerates such that 3,000 Joules of Work is performed. If the car travels 30 meters, how quickly did the car accelerate?

   A) 1 m/s^2
   B) 3 m/s^2
   C) 5 m/s^2
   D) 9 m/s^2

The correct answer is A:) 1 m/s^2. Using the equations: W=Fd, F=ma, then 3000=F(30) so F=100. And F=ma, therefore a=F/m=100/100= 1 m/s^2.

24) A 7 kg box falls off of a 3 meter shelf. When the box has fallen halfway to the ground, what forms of energy are present and in what amounts (ignore friction)?

   A) Elastic Potential = 21 Joules, Kinetic = 100 Joules
   B) Gravitational Potential = 102.9 Joules, Kinetic = 102.9 Joules
   C) Kinetic = 102.9 Joules, Normal = 21 Joules
   D) Gravitational Potential = 21 Joules, Kinetic = 21 Joules

The correct answer is B:) Gravitational Potential = 102.9 Joules, Kinetic = 102.9 Joules. At the top of the shelf the total gravitational potential energy will equal (m)(g)(h) = (7)(9.8)(3)= 205.8 Joules. That same amount of energy will have to be conserved according to the laws of thermodynamics. Therefore, when the box has fallen halfway to the floor, half of the energy will be gravitational potential, and half will be kinetic. 205.8/2=102.9.

25) Which of the following is NOT true based on Einstein's Special Theory of Relativity?

   A) The laws of physics are equally applicable in all frames of reference
   B) Light travels at a constant speed regardless of an objects motion
   C) A person traveling at the speed of light experiences time the same as a still person
   D) The relativity of space is explained by length contraction

The correct answer is C:) A person traveling at the speed of light experiences time the same as a still person. The theory of relativity is directly contrary to this. Rather, time is relative, and as a person draws nearer to the speed of light they will experience time more slowly.

26) According to the Special Theory of Relativity, which two measures are equivalent?

   A) Energy and speed
   B) Time and mass
   C) Speed and time
   D) Mass and energy

The correct answer is D:) Mass and energy. The concept of mass-energy equivalence is described by Einstein's famous equation: $E=mc^2$. In the equation E represents energy, m represents mass, and c represents the speed of light. Essentially the equation shows that mass and energy are directly related to each other at a ratio equal to the speed of light squared.

27) Which of the following is true about light?

   A) All light can be seen by the naked eye
   B) Light requires a medium to travel
   C) Objects with mass cannot travel the speed of light
   D) None of the above

The correct answer is C:) Objects with mass cannot travel the speed of light. Einstein stated that the speed of light is the upper boundary for the speed at which an object can travel. No object with mass can travel at the speed of light or else its mass would disappear as its length contracted.

CELESTIAL SYSTEMS

28) How did Earth come to have oxygen in its atmosphere?

   A) It always existed within the solar system and was drawn to the Earth because of its gravitational field.
   B) A giant meteorite that crashed into the Earth at some point in its development brought with it an abundance of oxygen molecules that then bound to the Earth's atmosphere.
   C) Through the presence of cyanobacteria that generate oxygen as a natural byproduct.
   D) None of the above.

The correct answer is C:) Through the presence of cyanobacteria that generate oxygen as a natural byproduct. Cyanobacteria are essentially the precursors to the organelles known as chloroplasts that make photosynthesis possible in plants today. Little is known about what caused them, but their generation of oxygen is what allowed further life to develop.

29) How old is the Earth?

   A) 2 billion years
   B) 4.5 billion years
   C) 6 billion years
   D) 10 billion years

The correct answer is B:) 4.5 billion years. The majority of the solar system all began forming at the same time, when the sun began developing into a star. Based on meteorite studies, the approximate age of the Earth has been determined to be 4.5 billion years.

30) The North Star has a declination of how many degrees?

   A) +90 degrees
   B) -45 degrees
   C) 0 degrees
   D) -90 degrees

The correct answer is A:) +90 degrees. Bodies that are located above the northern hemisphere, meaning those which are north of the equator, will have declinations ranging between zero and +90 degrees. Because it is nearly right above the North Pole, the North Star has a declination of +90 degrees.

31) A star that is located over the equator would have a declination of?

   A) +90 degrees
   B) +45 degrees
   C) 0 degrees
   D) -90 degrees

The correct answer is C:) 0 degrees. The celestial equator lines up with the Earth's equator. Just as the Earth's equator is 0 degrees latitude, the celestial equator is identified as 0 degrees.

32) The sun's orbit varies throughout the year, such that it appears at different locations in the night sky depending on the month. This cycle is known as the

   A) Ecliptic
   B) Declination
   C) Ascension
   D) Celestial pattern

The correct answer is A:) Ecliptic. In terms of the sun's position relative to the earth, the changes occur because the earth is tilted on an axis of 23.5 degrees relative to the sun. This causes position of the sun to appear to move across the backdrop of the celestial sphere. The path that it takes is known as the ecliptic.

33) When the moon is positioned between the Earth and the sun, what phase will it be in?

   A) First quarter moon
   B) New moon
   C) Full moon
   D) Last quarter moon

The correct answer is B:) New moon. In this position the half of the moon that is illuminated by the sun will be entirely facing away from the Earth, making it appear as though there is no moon at all. This is a new moon.

34) When the Earth is positioned directly between the sun and the moon, which of the following will occur?

   A) Solar eclipse
   B) Spring tide
   C) Tidal locking
   D) Lunar eclipse

The correct answer is D:) Lunar eclipse. The Earth's shadow will be cast over the moon, obscuring it. However, generally red light waves will shift around the Earth, and still be able to reach the moon, so it often won't completely disappear.

35) When the moon and the sun are on the same side of the earth, which tide will be created?

   A) Neap tide
   B) Spring tide
   C) Tidal locking
   D) Low tide

The correct answer is B:) Spring tide. The combined gravitational pulls of the moon and the sun will cause a higher than normal tide. It's called a spring tide because the water "springs" up more than it usually does. This happens once a month.

36) A neap tide is created when?

   A) The sun and moon are both visible in the sky at the same time
   B) The sun and moon are on opposite sides of the Earth
   C) The sun and moon are on the same side of the Earth
   D) The sun and moon are perpendicular relative to the Earth

The correct answer is D:) The sun and moon are perpendicular relative to the Earth. This means that the two will be pulling the oceans in different directions, causing the tide to be less severe than it normally is.

37) How long does it take for the Earth to complete a full orbit around the sun?

   A) 24 hours
   B) 28 days
   C) 52 days
   D) 365 days

The correct answer is D:) 365 days. The time it takes for a planet to orbit around the sun is called a year. The Earth does this once approximately every 365 days.

38) The variations in season are a result of?

   A) The Earth's axial tilt
   B) The excess buildup in greenhouse gasses at certain times of year
   C) The eccentricities in the Earth's orbit
   D) Changing geothermal forces from the Earth's core

The correct answer is A:) The Earth's axial tilt. Because of the Earth's axis, different hemispheres are tilted nearer and closer to the sun depending on what part of its orbit it is in. This is the main factor in causing the seasons.

39) When the sun is at its northernmost point on the celestial coordinate system, what phenomenon will occur on Earth (for the Northern Hemisphere)?

   A) Summer Solstice
   B) Winter Solstice
   C) Vernal Equinox
   D) Autumnal Equinox

The correct answer is A:) Summer Solstice. The Earth will reach its furthest point from the sun during the summer each year. At this time, its axial tilt will place the North Pole at its closest to the sun. The result of these two factors means that the sun will reach its northernmost point on the celestial coordinate system, and it will be the longest day of the year.

40) During a lunar eclipse, how will the moon appear?

   A) White
   B) Blue
   C) Red
   D) Not at all

The correct answer is C:) Red. As the light from the sun hits the Earth's atmosphere, the red colored light is redirected around the Earth and towards the moon. Other colors are either absorbed by the atmosphere, or are not redirected at the right angle so as to intersect with the moon. This results in its red color during a full lunar eclipse.

41) The point of zero Right Ascenscion is determined by the position of the sun during the?

   A) Summer Solstice
   B) Vernal Equinox
   C) Winter Solstice
   D) Autumnal Equinox

The correct answer is B:) Vernal Equinox. As the sun moves in its relative position on the celestial sphere, each month it is near a different constellation in the zodiac. Each year on the two equinoxes the sun will line up perfectly over the equator. The point where this crossover occurs in the spring – the Vernal Equinox – is set as the standard for measuring right ascension.

42) Which of the following is the reason that the same side of the moon always faces the Earth?

   A) Tidal locking
   B) Ecliptic orbits
   C) Right ascension
   D) Declination

The correct answer is A:) Tidal locking. When a planet is tidally locked to another its rate of rotation is the same as its orbit. In the moon's case both its rotation about the earth and its rotation about its own axis are slightly longer than 27 days. This results in the same side of the moon always facing the Earth.

THE SCIENCE OF LIGHT

43) Which of the following electromagnetic waves are entirely unable to penetrate the Earth's atmosphere?

   A) Visible light
   B) Gamma rays
   C) Radio waves
   D) Micro waves

The correct answer is B:) Gamma rays. Gamma rays are the highest frequency electromagnetic waves that have yet been detected. They cannot be viewed using mirrors or telescopes like normal light waves, but they are entirely absorbed by the Earth's atmosphere.

44) Why must X-rays be observed from space?

   A) They are invisible when they are heated by the Earth's surface
   B) They can't penetrate the atmosphere
   C) They can only travel short distances
   D) They are stronger further from the Earth's surface

The correct answer is B:) They can't penetrate the atmosphere. A majority of ultraviolet rays, and all x-rays and gamma rays are absorbed by the earth's atmosphere. This makes them visible only by objects outside the Earth's atmosphere.

45) Which of the following is NOT a wave on the electromagnetic spectrum?

   A) Sound waves
   B) Micro waves
   C) Radio waves
   D) Gamma rays

The correct answer is A:) Sound waves. Sound waves are a form of mechanical wave – they require a medium (such as air) to travel through. Light waves are able to rapidly travel through space because they do not require a medium.

46) Which quality of waves determines whether or not it is visible to the human eye?

   A) Direction of travel
   B) Equilibrium position
   C) Amplitude
   D) Frequency

The correct answer is D:) Frequency. The human eye is designed to interpret certain frequencies of light –we call this the visible light spectrum. The frequency of a light wave is the determining factor in establishing its properties, and what category of the electromagnetic spectrum it falls in.

47) What is the speed of light?

   A) 186 thousand m/s
   B) 100 million m/s
   C) 300 million m/s
   D) 9 trillion m/s

The correct answer is C:) 300 million m/s. This means that in a single year light can travel more than 9.5 trillion kilometers.

48) A parsec is approximately how far?

   A) 1 light year
   B) 3.2 light years
   C) 100 light years
   D) Half the distance to the sun

The correct answer is B:) 3.2 light years. Parsec stands for the parallax of an arc second. Essentially, a measurement of the star's location is taken at two different points in time. The Earth's movement during that time causes it to appear in a different location. A parsec is the distance away that a star would be if the angle of its apparent movement were one arc second.

49) Which type of electromagnetic wave provides evidence of the Big Bang Theory?

   A) Radio waves
   B) Infrared waves
   C) Ultraviolet waves
   D) Micro waves

The correct answer is D:) Micro waves. A low-energy background radiation in the form of micro waves fills the universe, and it seems to come from all directions with the same intensity, which made it highly unlikely that it was from any sort of local receiver. This supports the Big Bang theory because only a cosmic event as encompassing as the Big Bang could have generated so much radiation at such consistent levels throughout the universe.

50) Which of the following is an example of refraction?

   A) Mirrors
   B) Rainbows
   C) Asphalt heating more quickly than plastic
   D) Light bending around a black hole

The correct answer is B:) Rainbows. Refraction is light distortion that occurs when light changes mediums. For example, when light passes through a prism it will fan out – such as how light refracting through raindrops creates a rainbow in the sky.

51) What is the longest form of electromagnetic wave?

   A) Gamma rays
   B) Micro waves
   C) Radio waves
   D) Visible light

The correct answer is C:) Radio waves. The order from longest to shortest wavelengths is: radio waves, micro waves, infrared waves, visible light, ultraviolet light, x-rays, and gamma rays.

52) Infrared radiation is commonly observed in what form?

A) Sound
B) Gravity
C) Heat
D) Color

The correct answer is C:) Heat. All objects with a temperature greater than absolute zero emit some infrared radiation proportional to how warm they are. Some objects are hot enough that the heat manifests visibly, such as coals and fire. But even a person, animal, or block of ice will emit infrared light. This is advantageous to astronomers wishing to study objects that are too cool or distant to study within the visible light spectrum.

53) Ultraviolet light is useful for?

A) Understanding how galaxies progress through various stages and mapping interstellar clouds
B) Classifying stars and determining star compositions
C) Studying objects to cool to emit more low energy forms of light
D) Capturing images and determining temperature, wind speed, and other storm qualities

The correct answer is A:) Understanding how galaxies progress through various stages and mapping interstellar clouds. Ultraviolet rays don't penetrate through clouds, dust, or atmospheres well. The low penetration of ultraviolet light makes it ideal for mapping interstellar clouds and dust. It is also used to study more about the sun's atmosphere and surface conditions.

54) Which spectrum shows only the hottest and most active elements of the solar system such as black holes and neutron stars?

A) Radio
B) Visible
C) Infrared
D) Gamma

The correct answer is D:) Gamma. Gamma rays are the highest frequency electromagnetic waves that have yet been detected. Only active, high-energy elements of the universe are able to produce them.

55) Which of the following is NOT a type of spectra studied in spectroscopy?

- A) Continuous
- B) Secretion
- C) Emission
- D) Absorption

The correct answer is B:) Secretion. Continuous, emission and absorption are the three types of spectral signatures that can be created as light bends through a prism.

56) A continuous spectra is emitted by?

- A) Heated gasses
- B) Extremely cooled liquids
- C) Heated solids surrounded by cool gasses
- D) Blackbodies

The correct answer is D:) Blackbodies. Continuous spectra are typical of solid or liquid objects when heated – for example, people emit continuous spectra in the infrared range. In astronomic terms, an object that emits a continuous spectrum is known as a blackbody. Blackbodies are objects that perfectly absorb all light. As the blackbody is heated it will emit electromagnetic waves in a continuous spectrum based on the temperature it is heated to.

57) If a planet is said to have a blue-shift, what does this mean?

- A) It is moving towards the Earth
- B) It is not moving relative to the Earth
- C) It is rotating counterclockwise
- D) It is moving away from the Earth

The correct answer is A:) It is moving towards the Earth. Because the planet is moving towards the Earth, its light waves are slightly compressed, making them shift towards the blue end of the visible spectrum. This is not the case for the majority of objects in the universe.

PLANETARY SYSTEMS: OUR SOLAR SYSTEM AND OTHERS

58) Which planet does not have rings?

   A) Saturn
   B) Uranus
   C) Jupiter
   D) Venus

The correct answer is D:) Venus. While none of the terrestrial planets contain rings, each of the gas and ice giants have several.

59) Which of Jupiter's moons is known for its volcanic activity?

   A) Io
   B) Ganymede
   C) Callisto
   D) Europa

The correct answer is A:) Io. The moon Io is unique because it is the most volcanically active body in the solar system and one of the few moons to have volcanic activity at all.

60) What is the main component of Mars' atmosphere?

   A) Carbon Dioxide
   B) Helium
   C) Hydrogen
   D) Nitrogen

The correct answer is A:) Carbon Dioxide. Mars, like Venus, has a very thin atmosphere composed primarily of carbon dioxide (more than 95%). This makes it an unlikely candidate to support life. Its thin atmosphere makes Mars susceptible to dangerous dust storms.

61) The asteroid belt is between which two planets?

   A) Earth and Mars
   B) Mercury and Venus
   C) Mars and Jupiter
   D) Jupiter and Saturn

The correct answer is C:) Mars and Jupiter. The asteroid belt comprises the region that lies between the orbits of Mars and Jupiter, separating the terrestrial planets from the gas-based planets. It is more specifically referred to as the Main Belt to differentiate it from other asteroid clusters within the solar system.

62) Which of the following does NOT have a natural satellite?

   A) Mercury
   B) Mars
   C) Saturn
   D) Neptune

The correct answer is A:) Mercury. Mars has two moons, Saturn has 62, and Neptune has 13. Mercury and Venus are the only two planets with no moons (natural satellites).

63) The average temperature of Venus is?

   A) 850 F/450 C
   B) 700 F/400C
   C) 61 F/16 C
   D) -80 F/-60 C

The correct answer is A:) 850 F/450 C. Venus has the highest average temperature of any planet, even though it is further from the sun than Mercury. Its thin atmosphere and relative closeness to the sun expose it to incredible amounts of heat.

64) Which of the following isn't part of the solar system?

   A) Io
   B) Main Belt
   C) Local Group
   D) Triton

The correct answer is C:) Local Group. The Local Group is the name for a cluster of galaxies that the Milky Way galaxy belongs to.

65) What is the approximate age of the sun?

   A) 1 million years
   B) 2 billion years
   C) 4.5 billion years
   D) 13 billion years

The correct answer is C:) 4.5 billion years. Astronomers can estimate the age of a star based on its relative composition of hydrogen and helium. Our sun is a main sequence star approximately 4.5 billion years old.

66) The sun will ultimately turn into which of the following?

   A) Main sequence star
   B) Black hole
   C) Supernova
   D) White dwarf

The correct answer is D:) White dwarf. The sun doesn't have sufficient mass to evolve into a black hole or a supernova. After it burns through its hydrogen fuel, and progresses through the red giant phase, it will settle as a white dwarf cooling over a period of billions of years.

67) What is a flare?

   A) Spikes of solar material ejected from the chromosphere
   B) An explosion within the photosphere which ejects solar material into space
   C) Clouds of solar material pulled into the air by magnetism
   D) Dense, highly magnetic spots within the photosphere

The correct answer is B:) An explosion within the photosphere which ejects solar material into space. Solar flares tend to emerge from areas around sunspots. A solar flare occurs when an explosion within the photosphere ejects great amounts of solar material into the air. The ejections are known as solar storms as they travel through space.

68) What is the sun's total expected lifespan?

   A) 12 billion years
   B) 8 billion years
   C) 5 billion years
   D) 100 million years

The correct answer is A:) 12 billion years. A star of the sun's mass will remain in the main sequence phase for approximately 10 billion years. Beyond that it will take another 2 billion for it to move through the red giant phase, and eventually morph into a white dwarf.

69) What is the main component of the sun?

   A) Magnesium
   B) Iron
   C) Hydrogen
   D) Helium

The correct answer is C:) Hydrogen. The sun is approximately 75% hydrogen, 23% helium, and 2% heavier metals.

70) Which of the following planets has the coolest average temperature?

   A) Saturn
   B) Mars
   C) Neptune
   D) Uranus

The correct answer is C:) Neptune. Neptune is the furthest planet from the sun, giving it the coolest average temperature of any of the planets, and earning it the nickname as an ice giant.

71) Which of the following has the most moons?

   A) Saturn
   B) Neptune
   C) Mars
   D) Earth

The correct answer is A:) Saturn. Saturn has 62 moons, Neptune has 13 moons, Earth has 1 moon, and Mars has 2.

72) Which of the following has the longest year?

   A) Mercury
   B) Neptune
   C) Venus
   D) Saturn

The correct answer is B:) Neptune. In addition to being the coldest planet, Neptune is also the planet with the longest year, 165 Earth years.

73) Which of the following is NOT visible to the naked eye?

   A) Uranus
   B) Saturn
   C) Jupiter
   D) Both A and B

The correct answer is A:) Uranus. Mercury, Venus, Jupiter, and Saturn are all visible to the naked eye. Uranus is the first planet distant enough that it cannot be seen without the aid of a telescope.

74) Which planet has an axial tilt of close to 90 degrees?

   A) Jupiter
   B) Neptune
   C) Venus
   D) Uranus

The correct answer is D:) Uranus. Uranus has an axial tilt of 98 degrees, which gives it the appearance of rolling perpendicular to all of the other planets. The most likely explanation for this dramatic tilt is a collision with an Earth-sized body at some point since its formation.

75) Which planet has a moon named Triton?

   A) Jupiter
   B) Saturn
   C) Neptune
   D) Uranus

The correct answer is C:) Neptune. As a moon, Triton has many unique features. It is the largest moon in the solar system with a retrograde movement – meaning it rotates opposite to the planet it orbits. Because of Triton's unique orbit, it will one day move close enough to Neptune to be torn apart by its gravity. Seasons have even been discovered on Triton.

76) Which two planets are known as ice giants?

   A) Uranus and Neptune
   B) Jupiter and Uranus
   C) Saturn and Neptune
   D) Jupiter and Saturn

The correct answer is A:) Uranus and Neptune. These two planets are essentially massive balls of ice and gas. They are similar to the gas giants, but a greater distance from the sun gives them a much colder temperature.

77) Which of the following is NOT a terrestrial planet?

   A) Earth
   B) Neptune
   C) Mars
   D) Venus

The correct answer is B:) Neptune. Neptune is considered an ice giant. The four terrestrial planets are the four planets closest to the sun.

OUR GALAXY AND OTHER GALAXIES: CONTENTS AND STRUCTURE

78) What type of galaxy is the Milky Way?

   A) Irregular
   B) Elliptical
   C) Regular spiral
   D) Barred spiral

The correct answer is D:) Barred spiral. The Milky Way is a barred spiral galaxy with four arms.

79) What is the most common galaxy type?

   A) Elliptical
   B) Irregular
   C) Regular spiral
   D) Barred spiral

The correct answer is A:) Elliptical. Elliptical galaxies are an older form of galaxy that emerges as stars age, and multiple galaxies collide. They are dimmer than spiral galaxies, so they aren't as easy to identify, but they are predicted to be the most common form of galaxy in the universe.

80) How far is the next closest star to the sun?

   A) 1 light year
   B) 4 light years
   C) 50 light years
   D) 93 light years

The correct answer is B:) 4 light years. The star is called Alpha Centauri.

81) What phase is the sun currently in?

   A) Main Sequence
   B) Red Giant
   C) Protostar
   D) White Dwarf

The correct answer is A:) Main Sequence. A star the sun's size will remain in the Main Sequence phase for around 10 billion years before exhausting its hydrogen fuel supply.

82) Which of the following characterizes red giant star?

   A) Extremely rapid rotation speed
   B) Regular emission of pulses of light
   C) Theorized future existence, although none have yet been discovered
   D) Helium fusion resulting in star expansion

The correct answer is D:) Helium fusion resulting in star expansion. The ending of hydrogen fusion allows gravitational pressures to pull the star inwards. This results in increasing pressures and temperatures at its core which generate helium fusion. As fusion renews, pressures again push outward causing the star to expand several times its original size.

83) Which of the following is NOT true of blue dwarfs?

   A) They begin as red dwarfs
   B) They are still only theoretical
   C) They expand and cool after hydrogen fusion
   D) They heat to very high temperatures

The correct answer C:) They expand and cool after hydrogen fusion. The theory behind blue dwarf stars is that once hydrogen fusion stops in a red dwarf star, rather than progressing to a red giant stage like main sequence stars, the star will maintain its size and increase in temperature instead.

84) A star that is too small to begin Hydrogen fusion, but still emits its own light, is called what?

   A) Red Dwarf
   B) Brown Dwarf
   C) Blue Dwarf
   D) White Dwarf

The correct answer is B:) Brown Dwarf. Brown dwarf stars are sometimes considered to be failed stars. The pressure levels in a brown dwarf star are never high enough to ignite hydrogen fusion at the core. Despite the lack of fusion, however, brown dwarfs are considered stars because they still generate their own light.

85) Type II supernova result in

   A) Black holes
   B) White dwarfs
   C) Blue giants
   D) Open clusters

The correct answer is A:) Black holes. They are caused when heavier elements begin building up at the star's core. The amount of pressure and heat at the core at this point causes it to begin to collapse under its own gravitational force and energy and light explode outwards in a supernova, ultimately ending as a black hole or neutron star.

86) Neutron stars develop because

   A) Supernovas in two stars at the same moment cause the surrounding matter to reorganize
   B) Gravitational forces during the supernova cause the protons to be blasted into space
   C) Under immense pressure, all of the protons and electrons fuse into neutrons
   D) A nearby black hole pulls all of the electrons from the core of the planet

The correct answer is C:) Under immense pressure, all of the protons and electrons fuse into neutrons. In neutron stars a star more massive than the sun undergoes a supernova explosion that generates so much pressure on the core that protons and electrons fuse. The pressure results in gravitational pulls billions of times the strength of Earth's.

87) What type of clusters are typically found in the arms of spiral galaxies?

   A) Population III clusters
   B) Globular clusters
   C) Closed clusters
   D) Open clusters

The correct answer is D:) Open clusters. Open clusters are smaller groupings of stars – typically in the hundreds. These stars are younger and brighter than the stars of globular clusters. Open clusters are found in the spiral arms of many galaxies, and are still forming within the spirals of the Milky Way Galaxy.

88) Stars that orbit uniformly in the main disc of the galaxy are known as

   A) Population I
   B) Population II
   C) Population III
   D) Population IV

The correct answer is A:) Population I. Population I stars are primarily younger and more metal rich stars. These stars are found in the main disc of the galaxy. Population I stars tend to have more uniform and circular orbits that keep them on the main plane of the galaxy. The stars are loosely bound together in open clusters.

89) Population II stars have a lower metal content because they are

   A) Younger
   B) Brighter
   C) Smaller
   D) Older

The correct answer is D:) Older. Population II stars were born in a time when heavier metals were scarcely found throughout the galaxy, leaving them without an abundance of these materials at the time of their formation.

90) A theoretical HR Diagram plots – temperature vs luminosity

   A) Temperature vs magnitude
   B) Temperature vs luminosity
   C) Luminosity vs magnitude
   D) Luminosity vs color

The correct answer is B:) Temperature vs luminosity. An HR Diagram that plots temperature against luminosity is called a theoretical HR Diagram. One which plots absolute magnitude against spectral type is called an observational HR Diagram or color-magnitude diagram.

91) Which spectral class is the hottest?

   A) O
   B) B
   C) A
   D) M

The correct answer is A:) O. The order of spectral classes from hottest to coolest is: O, B, A, G, B, K, M.

92) Spectral classes group stars based on their

   A) Color
   B) Mass
   C) Density
   D) Distance from earth

The correct answer is A:) Color. This classification takes advantage of the relationship between the temperatures of stars and the color that they appear as. The hottest stars appear whiter or bluer, and the cooler stars appear closer to red or orange.

93) White dwarves are found in what region of the HR Diagram – bottom left

   A) Top right
   B) Bottom right
   C) Bottom left
   D) Top left

The correct answer is C:) Bottom left. This portion of the diagram represents stars that have a high temperature, high absolute magnitude, and low luminosity.

94) Which of the following is NOT true of black holes?

   A) They develop when stars detonate in a supernova
   B) Only gamma radiation can escape from them
   C) They are composed of a singularity and an event horizon
   D) All of the above are true

The correct answer is B:) Only gamma radiation can escape from them. A black hole is a very dense region of space that exerts a powerful gravitational pull. They have such strong gravitational force that not even light is able to escape from them, and as a result they cannot be directly observed.

95) What types of black holes are believed to be at the center of most galaxies?

   A) Horizontal
   B) Light-emitting
   C) Stellar
   D) Supermassive

The correct answer is D:) Supermassive. There are two types of black holes: stellar and supermassive. Supermassive black holes are similar to stellar black holes, but they are much larger. Although their origins are unclear, what is known is that supermassive black holes lie at the centers of galaxies.

96) The focus point of a black hole is called what?

   A) Event Horizon
   B) Singularity
   C) Foci
   D) Centrum

The correct answer is B:) Singularity. The singularity of a black hole is the single point at which all of its mass is centered. All of the mass contained within a black hole is drawn to the singularity, and it continues to be drawn inwards towards it. Ultimately a black hole will move towards having an infinite mass concentrated at this single point.

97) Quasars are powered by

   A) Helium fusion
   B) Gamma radiation
   C) Black holes
   D) Binary systems

The correct answer is C:) Black holes. Quasars, or quasi-stellar radio sources, are formed when particles near the edges of the black hole are ejected away from the black hole in streams called jets that move outward for millions of light years above and below the supermassive black hole.

98) Pulsars are what?

   A) Rapidly rotating neutron stars
   B) Feeding black holes
   C) Two stars orbiting each other about a common center
   D) An object that absorbs and emits all spectra of radiation

The correct answer is A:) Rapidly rotating neutron stars. The intense magnetic field of these pulsars generates a beam of light that radiates outwards from the star, and creates the appearance of pulsing light each time it completes a rotation.

99) What astronomical bodies are distinguished by their coma and tail?

   A) Asteroids
   B) Quasars
   C) Type O stars
   D) Comets

The correct answer is D:) Comets. Comets and asteroids differ in the fact that comets possess a coma and a tail. A coma is a gaseous cloud that emerges around a comet as it passes closely to the sun. The two tails, a dust tail and a gas tail, are created as a result of radiation from the sun.

100) Which of the following is NOT a component of spiral galaxies?

   A) Halo
   B) Disc
   C) Singularity
   D) Bulge

The correct answer is C:) Singularity. Spiral galaxies are typically younger and shine brighter than other galaxy structures. They include three main components: a bulge, a disk, and a halo.

101) Which form of galaxy is typically the oldest?

   A) Barred Spiral
   B) Spiral
   C) Elliptical
   D) Irregular

The correct answer is C:) Elliptical. In addition to being less visually exciting than spiral galaxies, elliptical galaxies are generally older and dimmer.

102) Which of the following is NOT a standard candle?

   A) Spiral galaxies
   B) Cepheid variables
   C) Type I supernovae
   D) All of the above are standard candles

The correct answer is A:) Spiral galaxies. A standard candle is essentially any object with a known absolute magnitude. If the absolute magnitude of the object can be determined, then it is possible to calculate its apparent magnitude, and therefore its distance from the Earth.

THE UNIVERSE: CONTENTS, STRUCTURE AND EVOLUTION

103) The most popular theory about the origin of the universe is

   A) The Big Bang
   B) Expansion and Contraction
   C) Oscillation Theory
   D) Steady-State Theory

The correct answer is A:) The Big Bang. Although it isn't possible to see back to the creation of the universe, the existence of cosmic background radiation and continuing expansion of the universe make this the most widely accepted explanation.

104) What is the curvature of the universe?

   A) Positive
   B) Negative
   C) Flat
   D) Unknown

The correct answer is C:) Flat. Recent experiments have shown within .4% margin of error that the curvature of the universe is flat.

105) The cluster of galaxies within 5 million light years of ours is called the

    A) Milky Way
    B) Local Group
    C) Solar Cluster
    D) Triangulum Cluster

The correct answer is B:) Local Group. The Local Group is a small unit of around 50 galaxies which are bound together by a mutual gravitational attraction, including the Triangulum galaxy, Andromeda galaxy, and Milky Way.

106) Long, thin streams of superclusters that are draw together by gravity are known as

    A) Supercluster streams
    B) Voids
    C) Walls
    D) Filaments

The correct answer is D:) Filaments. Filaments are long threadlike structures where dense populations of superclusters gather together. Filaments can extend for hundreds of millions of lights years, with thicknesses of only several million light years.

107) The basic unit of large-scale structures in the universe are

    A) Filaments
    B) Voids
    C) Galaxies
    D) Clusters

The correct answer is C:) Galaxies. Galaxies form groups and clusters, which in turn form superclusters. Superclusters are then pulled together to form filaments and so forth.

108) Galactic sheets (or walls) generally have a thickness of only

   A) 20 million light years
   B) 2 million light years
   C) 200 thousand light years
   D) 20 light years

The correct answer is A:) 20 million light years. Galactic sheets span hundreds of millions of light years in length and width, but with thicknesses of only 20 million light years.

109) The pattern of many smaller objects merging again and again to form larger structures is

   A) Superclustering
   B) Hierarchical clustering
   C) Homogenization
   D) None of the above

The correct answer is B:) Hierarchical clustering. Each smaller formation is part of another larger formation, with the pattern continuing and spanning throughout the observable universe. This process is known as hierarchical clustering.

110) How large is the observable universe?

   A) 10 billion light years
   B) 35 billion light years
   C) 46 billion light years
   D) 92 billion light years

The correct answer is D:) 92 billion light years. The observable universe is the portion of the universe that we have been able to examine. This is mapped out in a 92 billion light year sphere extending with the Earth around the center.

111) What percentage of the universe is composed of dark matter?

A) 5%
B) 27%
C) 68 %
D) 75%

The correct answer is B:) 27%. Dark matter composes 27% of the observable universe, dark energy composes 68%, and baryonic matter composes the remaining 5%.

112) What is the most common element in the universe?

A) Carbon
B) Helium
C) Oxygen
D) Hydrogen

The correct answer is D:) Hydrogen. Hydrogen and Helium dominate the universe, with Hydrogen accounting for 73% of the elements in the universe, and Helium accounting for another 25% approximately.

LIFE IN THE UNIVERSE

113) How long after the Earth's creation did life begin developing?

A) Less than 100 million years
B) Around 1 billion years
C) 2 billion years
D) 3.5 billion years

The correct answer is B:) Around 1 billion years. These first organisms would have developed 3.8 billion years ago – just less than a billion years after the origin of the Earth. These single celled organisms would have been able to survive in environments that would be toxic to most life today.

114) What is the most accepted theory of the generation of life on earth?

   A) Big Bang
   B) Panspermia
   C) Chemical development
   D) None of the above

The correct answer is C:) Chemical development. The opposing theory is panspermia – that life came first from elsewhere in the universe. However, chemical development on Earth has been proven more likely.

115) The first multicellular organisms were

   A) Eukaryotic cells
   B) Fungi
   C) Animals
   D) Virus

The correct answer is A:) Eukaryotic cells. Endosymbiotic theory argues that specialization of life began when mitochondria cells entered a symbiotic relationship with eukaryotic cells.

116) Which of the following is NOT a likely candidate for life within the solar system?

   A) Titan
   B) Europa
   C) Enceladus
   D) Mercury

The correct answer is D:) Mercury. The four most probable locations for life in the solar system are Titan, Europa, Enceladus, and Mars.

117)   The Fermi Paradox notes that

   A) Life should be more prevalent in the universe than it is
   B) Other civilizations in the universe should have reached out to us, but they haven't
   C) Life should not exist on Earth, but it does
   D) None of the above

The correct answer is A:) Life should be more prevalent in the universe than it is. Physicist Enrico Fermi noted the overwhelming evidence that life should be able to develop in other regions of space, but was able to find no observable evidence of it. This is known as Fermi's Paradox.

 ## Test Taking Strategies

Here are some test-taking strategies that are specific to this test and to other DSST tests in general:
- Keep your eyes on the time. Pay attention to how much time you have left.
- Read the entire question and read all the answers. Many questions are not as hard to answer as they may seem. Sometimes, a difficult sounding question really only is asking you how to read an accompanying chart. Chart and graph questions are on most DANTES/DSST tests and should be an easy free point.
- If you don't know the answer immediately, the new computer-based testing lets you mark questions and come back to them later if you have time.
- Read the wording carefully. Some words can give you hints to the right answer. There are no exceptions to an answer when there are words in the question such as always, all or none. If one of the answer choices includes most or some of the right answers, but not all, then that is not the answer. Here is an example:

> The primary colors include all of the following:
> A) Red, Yellow, Blue, Green
> B) Red, Green, Yellow
> C) Red, Orange, Yellow
> D) Red, Yellow, Blue

Although item A includes all the right answers, it also includes an incorrect answer, making it incorrect. If you didn't read it carefully, were in a hurry, or didn't know the material well, you might fall for this.
- Make a guess on a question that you do not know the answer to. There is no penalty for an incorrect answer. Eliminate the answer choices that you know are incorrect. For example, this will let your guess be a 1 in 3 chance instead.

 ## What Your Score Means

Based on your score, you may, or may not, qualify for credit at your specific institution. The current ACE recommended score for this exam is 400. Your school may require a higher or lower score to receive credit. To find out what score you need for credit, you need to get that information from your school's website or academic advisor.

You lose no points for incorrect questions so make sure you answer each question. If you don't know, make an educated guess. On this particular test, you must answer 100 questions in 90 minutes.

Test Preparation

How much you need to study depends on your knowledge of a subject area. If you are interested in literature, took it in school, or enjoy reading then your study and preparation for the literature or humanities test will not need to be as intensive as that of someone who is new to literature.

This book is much different than the regular CLEP study guides. This book actually teaches you the information that you need to know to pass the test. If you are particularly interested in an area, or feel that you want more information, do a quick search online. We've tried not to include too much depth in areas that are not as essential on the test. It is important to understand all major theories and concepts listed in the table of contents. It is also important to know any bolded words.

Don't worry if you do not understand or know a lot about the area. With minimal study, you can complete and pass the test.

One of the fallacies of other test books is test questions. People assume that the content of the questions are similar to what will be on the test. That is not the case. They are only there to test your "test taking skills" so for those who know to read a question carefully, there is not much added value from taking a "fake" test. So we have constructed our test questions differently. We will use them to teach you new information not covered in the study guide AND to test your knowledge of items you should already know from reading the text. If you don't know the answer to the test question, review the material. If it is new information, then this is an area that will be covered on the test but not in detail.

To prepare for the test, make a series of goals. Allot a certain amount of time to review the information you have already studied and to learn additional material. Take notes as you study; it will help you learn the material. If you haven't done so already, download the study tips guide from the website and use it to start your study plan.

Legal Note

All rights reserved. This Study Guide, Book and Flashcards are protected under US Copyright Law. No part of this book or study guide or flashcards may be reproduced, distributed or stored in a retrieval system, or transmitted in any form or by any means, electronic, mechanical, photocopying, recording, or otherwise, without the prior written permission of the publisher Breely Crush Publishing, LLC.

DSST is a registered trademark of The Thomson Corporation and its affiliated companies, and does not endorse this book.

Ptolemaic solar system model	Constructed first observatory
First type of telescope	Equation for power of telescope
Kepler's First Law	F=ma
Newton's Law of Inertia	Einstein's Special Theory of Relativity

Tycho Brahe	A geocentric model of the solar system, with a balancing point called the "equant."
Focal length of the optical lens divided by focal length of the eyepiece.	Galileo's refraction telescopes with concave and convex lenses.
Newton's Second Law. Motion is proportional to the force acting on an object and the objects mass.	Planets in the solar system orbit in an elliptical pattern.
Time is relative, described in the equation $E=mc^2$. A person experiences time more slowly at the speed of light.	An object travelling through space will continue in the same manner unless another force acts on it.

Cause of oxygen in Earth's atmosphere	Age of the Earth
Declination of the north star	New moon
Spring tide	Year measurement
Cause of seasons	Highest frequency electromagnetic waves

Based on meteorite studies, the Earth is 4.5 billion years old.	Cyanobacteria generate oxygen as a natural byproduct.
Phase when the moon is positioned between the Earth and the sun.	+90 degrees.
The time it takes for a planet to orbit around the sun. The longest planet year is 165 Earth years.	Occurs when the moon and sun are on the same side of the earth. Their combined gravity cause a higher tide.
Gamma rays. They cannot be viewed using mirrors or telescopes and cannot penetrate Earth's atmosphere.	Axial tilt. Different hemispheres are tilted nearer and closer to the sun.

Speed of light	Parsec
Refraction	Electromagnetic spectrum order
Common cause of infrared radiation	Spectral signatures
Planets in blue-shift	Io

The parallax of an arc second, approximately 3.3 light years in length.	300 million m/s.
From longest to shortest: radio waves, micro waves, infrared waves, visible light, ultraviolet light, x-rays, and gamma rays.	Light distortion that occurs when light changes mediums (example: rainbows).
Continuous, emission and absorption are the signatures created as light bends through a prism.	Heat. All objects NOT at absolute zero emit infrared radiation proportional to their warmth.
Jupiter's moon, unique for its volcanically activity.	Are moving towards the Earth. Their light waves are compressed, which makes them shift towards the blue end of the visible spectrum.

Main component of Mars' atmosphere	**Main Belt**
Local Group	**Age of the sun**
Flare	**Main component of the sun**
Planet with the most moons	**Triton**

The asteroid belt between Mars and Jupiter. It separates the terrestrial and gas-based planets. 	Carbon Dioxide. Mars has a thin atmosphere of over 95% carbon dioxide. 
Based on relative levels of hydrogen and helium, it is 4.5 billion years old. 	A cluster of galaxies that the Milky Way galaxy belongs to. 
Hydrogen. The sun is approximately 75% hydrogen, 23% helium, and 2% heavier metals. 	Occurs when an explosion within the photosphere ejects great amounts of solar material into the air (solar storms). 
A moon that orbits Neptune. Triton is the largest moon in the solar system with retrograde movement; it has seasons.	Saturn has 62 moons. 

Ice giants	Milky Way galaxy type
Most common galaxy type	Closest star to the sun
Brown Dwarf	Result of type II supernova
Neutron stars	Population I star movement

The Milky Way is a barred spiral galaxy with four arms. 	Uranus and Neptune. These planets are essentially massive balls of ice and gas. 
Alpha Centauri, approximately 4 light years away. 	Elliptical. Elliptical galaxies are an older form of galaxy. They are dimmer than spiral galaxies. 
Black holes. Heavy elements build up at the star's core. The pressure causes it to collapse. 	"Failed" stars that emit light, but their pressure is too low for hydrogen fusion. 
Uniform and circular orbits that keep stars on the main plane of the galaxy bound in open clusters. 	A supernova caused protons and electrons fuse at a star's core resulting in an extreme gravitational pull. 

Order of spectral classes	Basis of spectral class
Singularity of a black hole	Most common element in the universe
First multicellular organisms	Four most likely locations for life in the Milky Way
Fermi Paradox	Percent of universe is dark matter

Color	From hottest to coolest is: O, B, A, G, B, K, M.
Hydrogen accounts for 73% of the elements in the universe.	The point at which all of its mass is centered. All mass contained is drawn to the singularity.
Titan, Europa, Enceladus, and Mars.	Eukaryotic cells.
27%	Life has the potential to be more common in the universe, but no evidence of it is observed.

www.ingramcontent.com/pod-product-compliance
Lightning Source LLC
Chambersburg PA
CBHW081828300426
44116CB00014B/2516